TEN
QUESTIONS
TO DIAGNOSE YOUR
SPIRITUAL
HEALTH

"Whether we consider our spiritual health to be robust or weak, Don Whitney's leadership through this self-diagnosis will almost inevitably move you to a higher spiritual plane. Whitney has given us several excellent books on the spiritual disciplines, but I believe this is the most helpful of his books to date. I personally felt my yearning for God intensify and then found expression in tangible growth as I applied Whitney's tests and comments to my own spiritual life. I commend it highly to all sincere Christian seekers."

—T.W. HUNT, author and speaker

"Donald Whitney asks us to interrogate our hearts before evaluating our actions to assess the health of our souls. However, the questions he supplies for this assessment not only help us examine our spiritual health, but in profound ways impart divine nutrition to all who dare to ask what he suggests."

—BRYAN CHAPELL, PH.D.,
president of Covenant Theological Seminary,
author of *Christ-Centered Preaching*

"Don Whitney has done it again! After already giving me three of the books I most frequently recommend to others, I think he's given me a fourth! This book poses the questions we need to ponder if we're to persevere in following Christ."

—MARK DEVER, pastor,
Capitol Hill Baptist Church,
author of *Nine Marks of a Healthy Church*

"Vance Havner, in his book *Repent or Else,* states that just as we are often too busy for a spiritual checkup, so the church is often too occupied to submit to a spiritual examination. In *Ten Questions to Diagnose Your Spiritual Health,* Dr. Whitney has given us something to do just that. This is not a book you read only once. For believers who long for Revival, these are questions to which we'll regularly return. What a tool to prepare the hearts of a congregation for the Lord's supper, or, Solemn Assemblies!"

—RON OWENS, author of *Return to Worship* and *They Could Not Stop the Music,* music and worship consultant for the International Mission Board, SBC

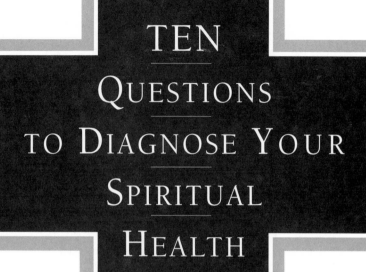

TEN
QUESTIONS
TO DIAGNOSE YOUR
SPIRITUAL
HEALTH

DONALD S. WHITNEY

NAVPRESS®

Bringing Truth to Life

OUR GUARANTEE TO YOU

The Navigators is an international Christian organization. Our mission is to advance the gospel of Jesus and His kingdom into the nations through spiritual generations of laborers living and discipling among the lost. We see a vital movement of the gospel, fueled by prevailing prayer, flowing freely through relational networks and out into the nations where workers for the kingdom are next door to everywhere.

NavPress is the publishing ministry of The Navigators. The mission of NavPress is to reach, disciple, and equip people to know Christ and make Him known by publishing life-related materials that are biblically rooted and culturally relevant. Our vision is to stimulate spiritual transformation through every product we publish.

© 2001 by Donald S. Whitney

All rights reserved. No part of this publication may be reproduced in any form without written permission from NavPress, P.O. Box 35001, Colorado Springs, CO 80935.
www.navpress.com

NAVPRESS, BRINGING TRUTH TO LIFE, and the NAVPRESS logo are registered trademarks of NavPress. Absence of ® in connection with marks of NavPress or other parties does not indicate an absence of registration of those marks.

ISBN 1-57683-096-9

Cover design by Ray Moore
Cover photos by RubberBall Productions
Creative Team: Greg Clouse, Deena Davis, Lori Mitchell, Pat Miller

Some of the anecdotal illustrations in this book are true to life and are included with the permission of the persons involved. All other illustrations are composites of real situations, and any resemblance to people living or dead is coincidental.

All Scripture quotations, unless otherwise indicated, are taken from the *New King James Version* (NKJV). Copyright © 1982 by Thomas Nelson, Inc. Used by permission. All rights reserved. Other versions used include: the *HOLY BIBLE: NEW INTERNATIONAL VERSION*© (NIV©), copyright © 1973, 1978, 1984 by International Bible Society, used by permission of Zondervan Publishing House, all rights reserved; the *New American Standard Bible* (NASB), © The Lockman Foundation 1960, 1962, 1963, 1968, 1971, 1972, 1973, 1975, 1977, 1995.

Whitney, Donald S.
    10 questions to diagnose your spiritual health / Donald S. Whitney.
        p. cm.
    Includes bibliographical references.
    ISBN 1-57683-096-9 (pbk.)
    1. Spirituality. I. Title: Ten questions to diagnose your spiritual health. II. Title.
BV4501.3 .W47 2001
248—dc21

                                                                    00-054822

FOR A FREE CATALOG OF
NAVPRESS BOOKS & BIBLE STUDIES,
CALL 1-800-366-7788 (USA)
OR 1-800-839-4769 (CANADA)

Printed in the United States of America
5 6 7 8 9 10 11 / 10 09 08 07 06

For "Him who is able to establish you . . . ; to the only wise God, through Jesus Christ, be the glory forever. Amen."
(Romans 16:25,27, NASB)

And for all three generations of my girls.
May the Lord always grant you
spiritual health and growth.

CONTENTS

ACKNOWLEDGMENTS

"First, I thank my God through Jesus Christ for you all" (Romans 1:8).

Much thanks to:

- Caffy and Laurelen, for your great patience. I love you.
- My brothers and sisters in Christ at North Pointe Baptist Church of Kansas City, for your prayers and encouragement. Your kindness repeatedly refreshed me, particularly during the last week of this project.
- My colleagues at Midwestern Baptist Theological Seminary, for your counsel and support.
- Nanci McAlister, for your consistent New Testament Christianity, even in "business," and for the "award."
- Sue Geiman, for your *long*-suffering.
- Kent Wilson, for your invitation to write the book.
- Mindy Rose, for your willing spirit on so many practical details.
- Mark and Sharon Coppenger, for the time invested to write two pages of ideas when I was stuck.
- Jim Orrick, for the creative recommendations and especially for your prayer that Wednesday night near the end.
- Rachel Sparks, for your typing. (And you, too, Jay, for running upstairs in the library late that night to help me complete that Spurgeon footnote.)
- Bob, Jenny, Josh, and Zach Hall, for your time and timely help. The food and the mowing made a hard time easier. And I wouldn't have made that flight if you hadn't printed the manuscript for me.

- Tammi Ledbetter, for finding a computer for me to use at the convention.
- The countless others who deserve thanks for their contribution to this book.

"For God is not unjust to forget your work and labor of love which you have shown toward His name, in that you have ministered to the saints, and do minister" (Hebrews 6:10).

INTRODUCTION

"During the past year, have you had any trouble sleeping? "Have you experienced any breathing difficulties? "Any changes in your eyesight? "Relax while I test your reflexes. "Has the nurse drawn your blood yet? "Now for this next test . . ."

This is the way it goes during my annual physical checkup. The doctor always evaluates my bodily health by two means— questions and tests.

The English Puritans of 1550 to 1700 used to refer to ministers as "physicians of the soul." In our day, as in theirs, the timeless process of discerning one's *spiritual* health likewise involves questions and tests. My purpose in writing these pages is to act as a physician of the soul—to ask questions and suggest spiritual tests that can, by the help of the Holy Spirit, enable you to self-diagnose your spiritual health.

For health to be present, of course, there must be life. I wrote this book with the assumption that its readers would possess the eternal life given by grace to those who know God through faith in His Son, Jesus Christ. The night before He was crucified, Jesus prayed, "And this is eternal life, that they may know You, the only true God, and Jesus Christ whom You have sent" (John 17:3). Stressing the necessity of knowing Jesus, the Son of God, in order to have eternal life, the apostle John added, "He who has the Son has life; he who does not have the Son of God does not have life" (1 John 5:12).

I realize, however, that many who begin reading here will do so with a false sense of assurance that they know Jesus and that God has given them eternal life. Nothing in the world is more important than an eternal, life-giving knowledge of God through Jesus, who is the only way to the Father (see John 14:6). I urge you not to take for granted the existence of such a relationship between yourself and God. The Bible itself implores you to "make your call and election sure" (2 Peter 1:10).

Where eternal life through Christ does exist, there should be not only health but also growth. That is what this book is about—evaluating your spiritual health and growth. Throughout, remember that just as Jesus is the source of spiritual *life,* so also is He the standard of spiritual *health.* And regarding spiritual *growth,* we are to "grow up in all things into Him who is the head—Christ" (Ephesians 4:15). As Jonathan Edwards said so emphatically,

> Christians are Christlike: none deserve the name of
> Christians that are not so, in their prevailing character
> . . . . The branch is of the same nature with the stock
> and root, has the same sap, and bears the same sort of
> fruit. The members have the same kind of life with the
> head. It would be strange if Christians should not be
> of the same temper and spirit that Christ is of; when
> they are his flesh and his bone, yea are one spirit
> (1 Corinthians 6:17), and live so, that it is not they
> that live, but Christ that lives in them.[1]

So whatever the present state of your spiritual health or the rate of your spiritual growth, let's begin by "looking unto Jesus, the author and finisher of our faith" (Hebrews 12:2), and "press toward the goal for the prize of the upward call of God in Christ Jesus" (Philippians 3:14). May the Lord be pleased to use this little volume to help you "grow in the grace and knowledge of our Lord and Savior Jesus Christ. To Him be the glory both now and forever. Amen" (2 Peter 3:18).

So holy desire, exercised in longings, hungerings, and thirstings after God and holiness, is
often mentioned in Scripture as an important
part of true religion.

—Jonathan Edwards

DO YOU THIRST
FOR GOD?

"Lord, I want to know You more," sang the soloist, just before
the sermon. One of my seminary professors from years back, who
was a guest preacher at our church that Sunday morning, sat next
to me on the front pew, transfixed. As the soloist continued, I could
hear my older friend sigh occasionally. When the song was over,
T. W. sat motionless for so long that I thought he had forgotten he
was now supposed to preach. As I turned to remind him, I saw his
shoulders lift and fall with the slow draw and release of his breath.
Finally, he opened his eyes and stepped thoughtfully to the pulpit.
He looked down for what seemed to be a full minute before he
could speak. And then he said, "Lord, I do want to know you more."
Departing from his prepared words for a while, he spoke of his
thirst for God, his longings to know Christ more intimately, to obey
Him more completely. Here was a man who had followed Christ

for more than fifty years and was still captivated by the sweetness of the quest. In his second half-century as a disciple of Jesus, the grace of growth still flourished in him.

It has been ten years since that Sunday morning. I've seen T. W. at least annually since then, and the things of God have not diminished their magnetic pull on his heart's aspirations. Two months ago I found myself sharing a shuttle bus ride with him from a denominational convention back to our hotel. Though nearly seventy now, and weakened by cardiac surgery, his eyes flashed as he talked for half an hour about what he was learning about prayer. Even as his body decays, his longings for God display the growing strength of his soul.

The apostle Paul must have similarly impressed others in his day. Despite his maturity in Christ and all he had seen and experienced, late in life Paul wrote of the passion that propelled him: "that I may know Him" (Philippians 3:10). What is he talking about? Didn't he already know Jesus more closely than perhaps anyone else ever would? Of course he did. But the more he knew Jesus, the more he wanted to know Him. The more Paul progressed in spiritual strength, the more thirsty for God he became.

With a similar thirst, the writer of Psalm 42:1-2 prayed, "As the deer pants for the water brooks, so pants my soul for You, O God. My soul thirsts for God, for the living God. When shall I come and appear before God?" Does this describe your thirst for God? If so, be encouraged; whatever else is transpiring in your Christian life, your soul-thirst is a sign of soul-growth.

THREE KINDS OF SPIRITUAL THIRST

Though it is not felt in every moment, in some sense there is a thirst in every soul. God did not make us to be content in our natural condition. In one way or another, to one degree or another, everyone wants more than he has now. The difference between people is the *kind* of thirsty longing in their soul.

THIRST OF THE EMPTY SOUL

The natural, that is, the unconverted man or woman, has an empty soul. Devoid of God, he is constantly in pursuit of that which will fill his emptiness. The range of his mad scramble may include money, sex, power, houses, lands, sports, hobbies, entertainment, transcendence, significance, or education, while basically "fulfilling the desires of the flesh and of the mind" (Ephesians 2:3). As Augustine attested, "Thou hast made us for Thyself, and our hearts are restless until they find their rest in Thee." Always searching and never resting, the empty soul turns from one pursuit to another, unable to find anything that will fill the God-shaped vacuum in his heart.

Thirsting and searching, the empty soul is blinded to his real need. Nothing or no one on earth fully and lastingly satisfies, but the empty soul doesn't know where to turn except to someone or something else "under the sun" (Ecclesiastes 1:9), as opposed to the One beyond the sun. Like Solomon, he discovers that no matter who or what he at first finds exciting, ultimately "all is vanity and grasping for the wind" (Ecclesiastes 1:14).

A Christian observes the man with the empty soul and knows that what he is looking for can be found only in the One who said, "whoever drinks of the water that I shall give him will never thirst" (John 4:14). Occasionally, an empty soul searches in more serious-minded or spiritual ways that lead some Christians to think he is thirsting for God. But the world has no such thirst. "There is none who understands," God inspired both King David and the apostle Paul to write, "there is none who seeks after God" (Psalm 14:2; Romans 3:11). Until and unless the Holy Spirit of God touches the spiritual tongue of the empty soul, that soul will never want to "taste and see that the Lord is good" (Psalm 34:8). Just because a man longs for something that can be found in God alone doesn't mean he's looking for God. A man may pine for peace yet have no interest in the Prince of Peace. Many who claim they are questing for

God are not thirsting for God as He has revealed Himself in Scripture, but only for God as they want Him to be, or for a god who will give them what they want.

The irony of the empty soul is that while he is perpetually dissatisfied in so many areas of his life, he is so easily satisfied in regard to the pursuit of God. His attitude toward spiritual matters is like that of the man who said to his complacent soul in Luke 12:19, "Soul, you have many goods laid up for many years; take your ease; eat, drink, and be merry." Whatever the empty soul may desire in life, he never has what the eighteenth-century pastor and theologian, Jonathan Edwards, called "holy desire, exercised in longings, hungerings and thirstings after God and holiness,"[1] as the Christian does.

The eternal tragedy is that if the empty soul never properly thirsts on earth, he will thirst in hell as did the rich man who pleaded in vain for even the tip of a moist finger to be touched to his tongue (Luke 16:24).

THIRST OF THE DRY SOUL

The difference between the empty soul and the dry soul is that one has never experienced "rivers of living water" (John 7:38), while the other has and knows what he's missing. That is not to say that the dry soul can lose the indwelling presence of the Holy Spirit; indeed, Jesus said, "the water that I shall give him will become in him a fountain of water springing up into *everlasting* life" (John 4:14, emphasis added).

How is it then that a true believer in Christ can become a dry soul when Jesus promised that "whoever drinks of the water I shall give him will never thirst" (John 4:14)?

Pastor and author John Piper was reading this verse one Monday morning and cried out, "What do You mean? I am so thirsty! My church is thirsty! The pastors whom I pray with are thirsty! O Jesus, what did You mean?"

As he meditated on the text, the illumination that seemed

to come from the Lord upon His Word was perceived by Piper this way:

> When you drink my water, your thirst is not destroyed forever. If it did that, would you feel any need of my water afterward? That is not my goal. I do not want self-sufficient saints. When you drink my water, it makes a spring in you. A spring satisfies thirst, not by removing the need you have for water, but by being there to give you water whenever you get thirsty. Again and again and again. Like this morning. So drink, John. Drink.[2]

A Christian soul becomes arid in one of three ways. The most common is by drinking too much from the desiccating fountains of the world and too little from "the river of God" (Psalm 65:9). If you drink the wrong thing it can make you even more thirsty. In particularly hot weather, my high school football coach would give us salt tablets to help us minimize the loss of fluids. During one game he experimented with stirring salt into our drinking water, hoping the diluted form would expedite the benefits of the salt. Bad idea. At halftime I drank until my stomach swelled and I was too heavy to run well, yet I was still thirsty.

Similarly, perhaps it was because the psalmist had drunk too much of the world's briny spiritual water that he wrote twice in one chapter about longing for God with all his heart while closely asserting his resolve not to wander from the Lord's Word (see Psalm 119:10,145). Too much attention to a particular sin or sins, and/or too little attention to communion with God (two things that often occur in tandem) inevitably shrivel the soul of a Christian.

Another cause of spiritual dryness in the child of God is what the Puritans used to call "God's desertions." While there are times when God floods our souls with a sense of His presence, at other times we dehydrate by a sense of His absence. Let me quickly say that His desertion of us is merely our *perception*, for the *reality* is just as Jesus promised: "I will never leave you nor forsake you" (Hebrews 13:5). When feeling deserted by God, however, the Christian believes himself to be in the valley of the shadow of death (Psalm 23:4), or somewhat like Jesus when He cried from the cross, "My God, My God, why have You forsaken Me?" (Matthew 27:46). The words of David in Psalm 143:6-7 describe the emotions of those who try to pray from such a spiritual desert: "I spread out my hands to You; my soul longs for You like a thirsty land. Answer me speedily, O LORD; my spirit fails! Do not hide Your face from me."

For reasons not always made clear to us, the Lord does sometimes withdraw a conscious sense of His nearness. Because this is not the place for a lengthy treatment of the subject,[3] the best concise counsel I can offer is that of William Gurnall: "The Christian must trust in a withdrawing God."[4] When the sun goes behind a cloud, it is no less near than when its rays are felt. However, for the specific purposes of this book and chapter, remember that it is a good thing that you are able to discern the seclusion of God's presence. Such spiritual sensitivity characterizes spiritual health.

A third cause of spiritual aridity in a Christian is prolonged mental or physical fatigue. Both the cause and the cure are usually obvious enough, so I won't elaborate on them. What I do want to emphasize is that a believer may not sense spiritual growth when fatigued or burned out, but instead may brood under shadowy thoughts about the reality of his relationship with Christ. And yet, much may have been learned in the very battle that caused the fatigue, things which, when the sunlight returns to the soul, will be seen as significant spiritual turning points. Again, don't forget that the longing for fresh water is itself a sign of progress.

Regardless of the cause, the dry Christian soul is like the

believer of Psalm 42:1-2, thirsting for God "as the deer pants for the water brooks." When you are in this condition, nothing else but the living water of God Himself will do. My daughter was three when she separated herself from me while we were in a child-oriented restaurant. She wanted to play with some of the game machines instead of eating. Though she had run to the far side of the restaurant, I could see her and was on my way to bring her back to the table. Suddenly she realized she didn't know where she was or where I was. Panic-stricken, she began crying and calling for me. At that moment, the store manager could have offered her unlimited play on every machine and given her every toy prize in the place, but nothing would have appealed to her without my presence. Everything else was meaningless to her without me. Once we were reunited, for a few moments she was content just for me to hold her, just to have me back. That's the cry of the dry soul. Other things may have distracted you, but now the only thing that matters is a return of the sense of your Father's presence.

THIRST OF THE SATISFIED SOUL

Unlike the dry soul, and as self-contradictory as it may sound at the moment, the satisfied soul thirsts for God precisely because he *is* satisfied with God. He *has* "taste[d] and see[n] that the LORD is good" (Psalm 34:8), and the taste is so uniquely satisfying that he craves more.

The apostle Paul personified this in his famous exclamation, "that I may know Him" (Philippians 3:10). In the preceding lines he had been exulting in his present knowledge of and relationship with Jesus. He announced, "But what things were gain to me, these I have counted loss for Christ. Yet indeed I also count all things loss for the excellence of the knowledge of Christ Jesus my Lord, for whom I have suffered the loss of all things, and count them as rubbish, that I may gain Christ" (verses 7-8). Then, just one verse later, the apostle cried out, "that I may know Him." Paul was soul-satisfied with Jesus Christ, yet thirsty for Him still.

Thomas Shepard, founder of Harvard University and an influential New England minister, explained the cycle of satisfaction and thirst this way: "There is in true grace an infinite circle: a man by thirsting receives, and receiving thirsts for more."[5]

Knowing Christ well is so spiritually thirst quenching because no person, possession, or experience can produce the spiritual pleasure we can find in Him. Communion with Christ is incomparably satisfying because there is no disappointment in what you find in Him. Moreover, the spiritual gratification you find in Him initially is never ending. On top of these, the Lord in whom this satisfaction is found is an infinite universe of satisfaction in which one may immerse himself to explore and enjoy without limitation. So there is no lack of satisfaction in knowing Christ, but neither has God designed us so that one experience with Christ satiates all future desire for Him.

Here's how Jonathan Edwards described the relationship between the spiritual good enjoyed in fellowship with Christ and the thirst for more that it produces:

> Spiritual good is of a satisfying nature; and for that
> very reason, the soul that tastes, and knows its nature,
> will thirst after it, and a fullness of it, that it may be
> satisfied. And the more he experiences, and the more
> he knows this excellent, unparalleled, exquisite, and
> satisfying sweetness, the more earnestly he will
> hunger and thirst for more.[6]

Has your worship or devotional experience lately provided you with ravishing tastes of what A. W. Tozer called the "piercing sweetness"[7] of Christ, only to leave you with a divine discontent that desires more? Would the following prayer of Tozer's reflect your own aspirations?

O God, I have tasted Thy goodness, and it has both satisfied me and made me thirsty for more. I am painfully
conscious of my need for further grace. I am ashamed of
my lack of desire. O God, the Triune God, I want to
want Thee; I long to be filled with longing; I thirst to be
made thirsty still.[8]

Such desires, Christian brother or sister, are marks of a growing soul.

THE BLESSING OF SPIRITUAL THIRST

"How blessed are all those who long for Him," declared the prophet
Isaiah (30:18, NASB). "Blessed are those," reiterated Jesus, "who
hunger and thirst for righteousness" (Matthew 5:6). A thirsting
desire for the Lord and His righteousness is a blessing. How so?

GOD INITIATES SPIRITUAL THIRST

The reason a person thirsts for God is because the Holy
Spirit is at work within him. If you are a Christian, two people
live in your body—you and the Holy Spirit. As the apostle Paul
explained, "Do you not know that your body is the temple of
the Holy Spirit who is in you, whom you have from God, and
you are not your own?" (1 Corinthians 6:19). And the Holy
Spirit is not passive within you.

For example, just as you can choose to put thoughts in your
consciousness, so can He, and He does. For instance, as you can
decide to think for a few moments about what you should do
this evening, so He can plant thoughts in your mind about God
and the things of God. Such work is part of how He causes a
Christian to be "spiritually minded" (see Romans 8:5).[9] Another
part of that ministry is to cause you to have Godward thirsts and
longings (such as "Abba, Father," see Romans 8:15), as well as
other signs of spiritual vitality.

23

Charles Spurgeon, the peerless British Baptist preacher of the 1800s, elaborated on the blessing of thirsting:

> When a man pants after God, it is a secret life within which makes him do it: he would not long after God by nature. No man thirsts for God while he is left in his carnal [that is, unconverted] state. The unrenewed man pants after anything sooner than God: . . . It proves a renewed nature when you long after God; it is a work of grace in your soul, and you may be thankful for it.[10]

GOD INITIATES SPIRITUAL THIRST IN ORDER TO SATISFY IT

God does not fire a thirst for Himself in order to mock us or frustrate us. He Himself declared, "I did not say to the seed of Jacob, 'Seek Me in vain'" (Isaiah 45:19). What is true for the physical lineage of Jacob (Israel) is also true for his spiritual descendants, in other words, those who believe in Israel's Messiah, Jesus. God creates a thirst for Himself so that He can satisfy it with Himself. "For He satisfies the longing soul," is the promise of Psalm 107:9, "and fills the hungry soul with goodness." Jesus assured us that "blessed are those who hunger and thirst for righteousness, for they *shall* be filled" (Matthew 5:6, emphasis added).

Jonathan Edwards argued that Scripture plainly teaches that "the godly are designed for unknown and inconceivable happiness."[11] And, "no doubt but God will obtain his end in a glorious perfection."[12] If God has indeed made us for an unimaginable fullness of joy and has implanted longings for it, then surely

> God has made man capable of exceeding great happiness, which he doubtless did not in vain. . . . To create man with a capacity that he never intended to fill, . . . would have been to have created a large capacity when there was need but of a smaller; yea, it makes man less

happy, to be capable of more happiness than he shall
ever obtain. . . . [C]an any think that man, . . . was
intended in his creation to be left in this respect
imperfect, and as a vessel both partly empty and never
to be filled? . . . It appears that man was intended for
very great blessedness, inasmuch as God has created
man with a craving and desire that can be filled with
nothing but a very great happiness. . . . God did not
create in man so earnest a desire, when at the same
time he did not create for so much as he should desire.
. . . [A] desire that could never be satisfied would be
an eternal torment.[13]

Edwards maintained, of course, that this "craving and desire"
was a Christian's thirst for God, a longing that can be thoroughly
and finally satisfied only in the eternal, undiminished, and face-
to-face enjoyment of the Lord Himself in Heaven. Therefore,
wrote Edwards,

Seeing that reason does so undeniably evidence that
saints shall, some time or other, enjoy so great glory,
hence we learn that there is undoubtedly a future state
after death, because we see they do not enjoy so great
glory in this world. . . . [A]ll the spiritual pleasure they
enjoy in this life does but enflame their desire and thirst
for more enjoyment of God; and if they knew that there
was no future life, [it] would but increase their misery,
to consider that after this life was ended they were never
to enjoy God anymore at all. How good is God, that he
has created man for this very end, to make him happy
in the enjoyment of himself, the Almighty.[14]

Once beholding His glory, believers will testify that "they are
abundantly satisfied with the fullness of Your house, and You
give them drink from the river of Your pleasures" (Psalm 36:8).

Do you thirst for God? Thirst is a God-planned part of the growth of a soul toward its heavenly home.

PRACTICAL STEPS FOR THIRSTING AFTER THE THIRST-SLAKER

If you possess a true thirst for God, you will long to long even more. As Edwards insisted, "True and gracious longings after holiness are no idle ineffectual desires."[15]

Meditate on Scripture. Note that we are to "meditate," not merely read. Many languishing souls are assiduous Bible readers. Without the addition of meditation, warned the great man of prayer and faith George Müller, "the simple reading of the Word of God" can become information that "only passes through our minds, just as water passes through a pipe."[16]

Think of the incessant flow of information through your mind on a daily basis—all that you see, read, and hear. Most of us struggle with "information overload," unable to keep up with the constant input of data. If we are not careful, the words of the Bible can become just another gallon of words in the ever-increasing current through our thoughts. As soon as they pass by, pushed on by the pressure of the flow in the pipe, we remember little (if anything) of what we've just read, for we must immediately shift our focus to what's now before us. So much processes through our brains; if we don't absorb some of it we will be affected by none of it. And surely if we should absorb anything that courses through our thinking, it should be the inspired words from Heaven. Without absorption of the water of God's Word, there's no quenching our spiritual thirst. Meditation is the means of absorption.

Spend 25 to 50 percent of your Bible intake time meditating on some verse, phrase, or word from your reading. Ask questions of it. Pray about it. Take your pen and scribble and doodle on a pad about it. Look for at least one way you could apply it or live it. Linger over it. Soak your soul slowly in the water of the Word, and you'll find it not only refreshes you, but prompts a satisfying thirst for more.[17]

Pray through Scripture. After you read through a section of Scripture, pray through part of that same passage. Whether you read one or many chapters of the Bible per day, afterward choose a portion of your reading and, verse by verse, let the words of God become the wings of your words to Him.

While it is possible to pray through any part of Scripture, I particularly recommend, regardless of where in the Bible you have done your reading, that you turn to one of the Psalms and pray your way through as much of it as you can. The book of Psalms was the God-inspired hymnbook of Israel. In addition, twice in the New Testament (see Ephesians 5:19 and Colossians 3:16) Christians are commanded to sing psalms. Unlike any other book of the Bible, the Psalms were inspired *by* God for the express purpose of being reflected *to* God.

Say, for example, you begin praying your way through Psalm 63. The first verse is: "O God, You are my God; early will I seek You; my soul thirsts for You; my flesh longs for You in a dry and thirsty land where there is no water." You could enter into prayer by confessing that the Lord is your God, graciously thanking Him for that, then simply exulting in God as God. Next you could express your soul's thirsts and longings for Him, acknowledging what a blessing it is to have a God-given thirst for God, and so on. Perhaps then you would ask the Lord to plant a God-thirst in your children, or in someone with whom you've been sharing the gospel. On you would go through the psalm, praying about whatever the text said and whatever occurs to you as you read it. If nothing comes to mind while pausing over a verse or section of verses, go on to the next.

The poetic, visceral, and spiritually transparent elements of the Psalms often combine in ways that send the soul soaring and inflame passion for God. They deal realistically with the full range of human emotions and can take you from wherever you are spiritually and lift you heavenward. Nothing so consistently renews my longings for God and catapults me into experiential communion with Him as praying through a psalm.

Read thirst-making writers. After the God-breathed words of the Bible, read the time-tested works of those Christian writers who wrote with a thirst-making pen. If you can find the collection of Puritan prayers and devotions called *The Valley of Vision*[18] you will be blessed by reading it meditatively. Don't neglect John Bunyan's classic *Pilgrim's Progress*. Read the more devotional pieces of Puritan writers such as John Owen, Richard Sibbes, Thomas Brooks, John Flavel, and Thomas Watson. Enjoy the books and sermons of Jonathan Edwards and of Charles Spurgeon for they will be treasured as long as the church is on the earth. For more recent publications, A. W. Tozer's small books are both convicting and exhilarating; John Piper's writings are a burning blend of spirit and truth.

As He has with my friend T. W., may the Lord bless you with a great and lifelong thirst for Himself, for surely He intends to satisfy it with Himself.

THE SUM AND SUBSTANCE OF THE PREPARATION NEEDED FOR A COMING ETERNITY IS THAT YOU BELIEVE WHAT THE BIBLE TELLS YOU AND DO WHAT THE BIBLE BIDS YOU.

ARE YOU GOVERNED INCREASINGLY BY GOD'S WORD?

WHAT DO YOU BELIEVE TO BE THE MOST VALUABLE TANGIBLE OBJECT in the world? Perhaps you think of something like the Hope Diamond, the *Mona Lisa,* Michelangelo's sculpture of David, or the gold burial mask of King Tut's tomb. As costly as these are, the price tag on some enormous skyscraper could be higher. And yet, offer any of these to an emaciated man who is hours from dying of thirst and hunger, and the relative value of the world's greatest treasures drops to nothing. Though inexpensive and often taken for granted, ultimately it is the basics of life—things such as food and water—that are most precious. For without them, there is no life at all.

Therefore, I submit that the single most valuable item on earth is the Bible. God's Word is like water, according to

Ephesians 5:26. It is also food. As the prophet Jeremiah said to God, "Your words were found, and I ate them, and Your word was to me the joy and rejoicing of my heart" (Jeremiah 15:16). Jesus Himself proclaimed that "man shall not live by bread alone, but by every word that proceeds from the mouth of God" (Matthew 4:4). It is true that without physical food our bodies would die in a matter of days. But without soul nourishment, we perish forever.

Food and water are essential, but there are other things basic to life, and the Word of God is compared to these as well. It is called a light (Psalm 119:105), a fire and a tool (Jeremiah 23:29), a weapon (Ephesians 6:17), and seed (1 Peter 1:23). Moreover, the Word of God is perfect, sure, right, pure, true and righteous, sweeter than honey, and to be desired more than much fine gold (Psalm 19:7-10). Indeed the psalmist exclaimed, "The law of Your mouth is better to me than thousands of coins of gold and silver" (Psalm 119:72). It can convert the soul, make wise the simple, rejoice the heart, and enlighten the eyes (Psalm 19:7-9). The Bible is unlike any other book, religious or secular, "for the word of God is living and powerful, and sharper than any two-edged sword, piercing even to the division of soul and spirit, and of joints and marrow, and is a discerner of the thoughts and intents of the heart" (Hebrews 4:12).

The written words of God are closely identified with God Himself. Through them He makes Himself most clearly known and declares to us the way to Himself through Christ. Without knowledge of God, no matter how long and prosperous one's earthly existence, life is meaningless and worthless. Thus no other object on earth is as valuable as the Bible, for nothing else can provide anything as essential or eternal.

Given the incomparable value of Scripture, the Christian's need for its constant influence cannot be overstated. God's Word is the manna by which the heavenly Father feeds His children so that they can grow more into the likeness of His perfect Son. That is why the Lord has told us to "desire the pure milk of the word, that you may grow thereby" (1 Peter 2:2).

While the Pharisees of Jesus' day and certain cult groups in our own are evidence that more is needed to become Christlike than megadoses of Scripture, still it is true that little input of God's Word results in little resemblance to God's Son. So one question by which you can evaluate your spiritual health and growth is, "Are you governed increasingly by God's Word?"

LIKE THE IMPRINT OF WORDS UPON THE AIR

Do you find yourself inquiring—consciously—how the Bible speaks to specific areas of life? Do you ask others, perhaps those in spiritual leadership or who are mature, to help you apply Scripture in particular situations? Is it your practice to actually turn the pages of the Bible in search of the will of God?

Many professing Christians bump along from Sunday to Sunday, year to year, with no recollection of changes in beliefs or practices as a result of new discoveries in the Word. They would tell you they believe the same as they did years ago. They carry a Bible to church, but they couldn't tell you the last time their daily life was altered by it. They may even be daily Bible readers, and they have heard one or more sermons per week for years. Yet with all their exposure to the Bible, generally its inspired words leave no more imprint upon their minds than spoken words do upon the air. It could never be said of them that they deliberately govern their daily lives by God's Word.

In his nineteenth-century book *Personal Declension and Revival of Religion in the Soul*, British minister Octavius Winslow further described those in this spiritual regression:

> When a professing [Christian] man can read his Bible
> with no spiritual taste, or when he searches it, not
> with a sincere desire to know the mind of the Spirit in

order to [walk] a holy and obedient walk, but with a merely curious, or literary taste and aim, it is a sure evidence that his soul is making but a retrograde movement in real spirituality. Nothing perhaps more strongly indicates the tone of a believer's spirituality, than the light in which the Scriptures are regarded by him. They may be read, and yet be read as any other book, without the deep and solemn conviction that "all Scripture is given by inspiration of God, and is profitable for doctrine, for reproof, for correction, for instruction in righteousness; that the man of God may be perfect, thoroughly furnished unto all good works" (2 Timothy 3:16-17). They may be read without a spiritual relish, without being turned into prayer, without treasuring up in the heart and reducing to daily practice its holy precepts, its precious promises, its sweet consolations, its faithful warnings, its affectionate admonitions, its tender rebukes.[1]

The person who can content himself with few or routine contacts with Scripture may be manifesting something far worse than spiritual decline. The Bible characterizes a genuine believer as not merely an admirer of God's truth, but one who *loves* it. The writer of Psalm 119 said repeatedly:

- And I will delight myself in Your commandments, which I love. (verse 47)
- My hands also I will lift up to Your commandments, which I love. (verse 48)
- Oh, how I love Your law! It is my meditation all the day. (verse 97)
- I hate the double-minded, but I love Your law. (verse 113)
- You put away all the wicked of the earth like dross; therefore I love Your testimonies. (verse 119)

- Therefore I love Your commandments more than gold, yes, than fine gold! (verse 127)
- I hate and abhor lying, but I love Your law. (verse 163)

Conversely, Scripture speaks of nonChristians as "those who perish, because they did not receive the love of the truth, that they might be saved" (2 Thessalonians 2:10). John Piper noted, "Loving the truth is a matter of perishing or being saved. Indifference to the truth is a mark of spiritual death."[2] Are you indifferent to the truth of Scripture? Are you in retrograde? Or does God's Word have a growing influence in your life?

You are reading this because you want to become more like Jesus Christ, right? What influence did Scripture have on *His* earthly life?

THE WORD GOVERNED BY THE WORD

Jesus, the Incarnate Word of God (John 1:1), was continually governed by the inscribed Word of God. Immediately prior to His emergence into public ministry came His baptism and then the temptation by Satan. In the furnace of that temptation, Jesus Christ went to Scripture alone. Repeatedly He repulsed the tempter's crafty beguilements with the words "It is written" (see Matthew 4:1-11).

Jesus might have reasoned, "Look, Satan, you know that I'm not only a man, I am God. Fully God. God cannot be tempted. You're wasting your time." He could have argued, "Don't you realize by now that you can't win?" or "My power is greater than yours." He might have challenged Satan to a contest of supernatural abilities, similar to the confrontation between Elijah and the prophets of Baal (see 1 Kings 18:20-40). Instead Jesus found all that He needed in what God the Father had spoken. For it was here that He hurled Deuteronomy 8:3

at His wicked enemy: "Man shall not live by bread alone, but by every word that proceeds from the mouth of God" (Matthew 4:4).

Throughout the Gospels we find Jesus quoting Scripture, often asking, "Have you never read?" He knew the Scriptures intimately. Why? Because He is God, the Author of the Scriptures? Yes, but too often we attribute Jesus' mastery of the Old Testament to His divinity. Though He was undiminished deity, Jesus quoted Scriptures He had memorized as a *man*, learning them from childhood in the same kinds of ways people like ourselves can.

As it was for Jesus, it is normal for Jesus' followers to be governed by Scripture. And those who are becoming more like Jesus will, over time, live more and more "by every word that proceeds from the mouth of God."

"TO THE LAW AND TO THE TESTIMONY!"

The prophet Isaiah lived in a time not unlike our own. People commonly sought answers in all the wrong places. "To the law and to the testimony!" the prophet directed his hearers (Isaiah 8:20). "If they do not speak according to this word," he warned, "it is because there is no light in them." In other words, if people's lives aren't guided by God's revelation, it's because they are in spiritual darkness. The light of God's Spirit has never dawned within them.

As Spirit-indwelled people grow to resemble Jesus more and more, they should think more quickly and more often, "To the law and to the testimony!" This means immediately asking yourself, "What does the Bible say?" when dealing with even the most common issues, whenever you have a question about *anything*.

How should my child be educated? How would God have me vote in this political election? Should I make this purchase? What are the right reasons for choosing a church? Is this man qualified to be our new pastor? How should our church—and I—reach people with the gospel? How much time at my job is too much? What should I do with my life when I retire from my career? All of life—events and choices great or small—should be governed by the Word of God.

To live this way requires the constant consultation of Scripture. And this is exactly what the well-known words of Psalm 119:105 imply: "Your word is a lamp to my feet and a light to my path." Wherever we go, whatever decisions are before us, the way of life should be illuminated by God's Word. To live otherwise is to walk in darkness.

No Christian, of course, always and perfectly lives in accordance with Scripture. Only Jesus has done that. So we speak of being governed by Scripture as (1) a general characteristic of a true follower of Jesus, and yet (2) something that *increasingly* characterizes the growing Christian. Speaking in a practical way, you know that God's Word is growing in its influence over you when you can point to increasing numbers of beliefs and actions that have been changed because of the potency of specific texts of Scripture. You can recall times when, like Apollos in Acts 18:26, you realized that you held to doctrinal error and then changed your position as you saw "the way of God more accurately." You remember various turning points where you stopped or started some action or habit as a result of a new understanding of biblical truth.

One testimony of this in my own life has been mentioned already (at the end of chapter 1), namely, how the Bible has increasingly governed my prayer life as I have let the words of God, and especially the Psalms, give direction to my prayers.

Here is another. During my first nineteen years of pastoral ministry, I purposelessly evaluated what was or was not appropriate for worship based more upon personal preference, expedience, and "Will anyone be offended by this?" than upon what Scripture said. If I could think of nothing in the Bible against what I was considering, I assumed it was acceptable for worship. I began to see that a more deliberately biblical way of being governed by God's Word is to look for a positive indication from Scripture that the proposed element should be a part of public worship. So rather than asking, "Is there anything in the Bible *forbidding* it?" I have learned to ask, "Is there any biblical command, example, or sanction *supporting* this activity in worship?" This made a difference, for instance, in giving me intentionality about singing more psalms in worship (see Ephesians 5:19 and Colossians 3:16) than I had previously.

One more example of how the Lord has been reshaping my life to conform more to His Word has to do with my beliefs and practice about the Lord's Day. Most conservative, Bible-believing Christians I know seem to make few choices about their Lord's Day activities based on Scripture. Rather they base their choices on their culture—their family culture, church culture, or the culture of society at large. So whether they go to the mall, watch football, play golf, eat out, take a nap, work in the yard, or whatever, they do what they do more because of the traditions of their family, church, or community than because of what the Bible says. If everyone in the church talks about and watches the big NFL game on Sunday, they probably will too. Or if they do not watch the game, it's only because they don't like football or they have something else they would rather do or must do. Regardless, the decision is not made consciously for biblical reasons.

As I examined the Scriptures pertaining to this issue, my habits on the Lord's Day were transformed. The Bible has directed me on this matter in ways that are refreshing, restorative, and recreative for my soul, mind, body, and family. In summary, I have understood the Bible to teach that my greatest privilege and first responsibility on the Lord's Day is to worship Him with His people. Also, because the first day of the week is called in Scripture "the Lord's Day" (Revelation 1:10), the day should be observed uniquely for the Lord, and every activity should be evaluated by that fact. However *you* choose to spend the Lord's Day, I appeal to you to base your decisions and actions on the revelation of God.

The Bible should be the measure and evaluator of all things in the life of every believer. God categorically claims that His Word can equip us for *every* good work: "All Scripture is given by inspiration of God, and is profitable for doctrine, for reproof, for correction, for instruction in righteousness, that the man of God may be complete, thoroughly equipped for every good work" (2 Timothy 3:16-17). Here are some ways you can begin to prove this enormously important truth.

DEVELOPING YOUR DEPENDENCE ON GOD'S WORD

Deepen your desire for God's Word. Do you "desire the pure milk of the word, that you may grow thereby" (1 Peter 2:2)? Without spiritual food there is no spiritual growth. And one of the best ways for acquiring a taste for God's food and cultivating this Spirit-given appetite is simply to discipline yourself to feast on it. Nothing can make us hungry for Scripture more than Scripture itself.

For starters, make sure you are in a church with heartfelt, conscience-stirring preaching that clearly comes from the pages of Scripture. At this point in my life I preach in a different church almost every Lord's Day. In some towns I ask myself, "What would I do if I lived here?" for it is evident that a famine of God's Word exists there. Maybe you live in such a place. You've had the same sparse spiritual diet from the pulpit for so long that even though you are starving, you're almost too spiritually weak to take action. Don't give up and don't fail to assume responsibility. Seek out good nourishment through radio, tapes, CDs, audio over the Internet, and so forth.

Let me say again that praying through Scripture is an excellent way to rekindle a craving for it. And once more, don't simply read the Bible, *meditate* on it. Choose at least one verse from your reading and think about it. What do the words tell you about Christ? How can you experience deeper communion with Him because of what's written there? For what situation or person could you use the passage as a basis of prayer? Try rewriting the verse in your own words. Find at least one way you could apply it. Read less, if necessary, in order to meditate more. There are astonishing promises attached to the meditation of Scripture (see Joshua 1:8; Psalm 1:1-3; James 1:25). What praying through Scripture can do to reinvigorate your prayer life, meditation on Scripture can do to revitalize all forms of your Bible intake.

And if you want guidance specifically regarding the *desire* for God's Word, pray through or meditate on Psalm 119 until you believe that your own heart is represented in that glorious chapter. Let the God-breathed words of that passage breathe the freshest of air into your soul.

Make time for God's Word. If you can't do this, you aren't dependent on Scripture—and never will be. Just as we schedule times to eat our physical food, so we must do the same for our spiritual food. From this moment forward, adopt as your own the resolution of Jonathan Edwards: "Resolved, To study the Scriptures so steadily, constantly, and frequently, as that I may find and plainly perceive myself to grow in the knowledge of the same."[3]

Read the Bible daily and do not close it until you know at least one thing God would have you do in response to your reading. This response might involve something new to believe, a habit to begin or break, a prayer to offer, a conversation to initiate, a letter or E-mail to send, a phone call to make, a spiritual discipline to practice, or something else. Read the Bible for application, not merely for information.

List at least five areas you have not recently considered from a biblical perspective. Then search the Scriptures and prayerfully consider one area each day for the next five days. Here are five major areas or segments of life, with ten categories under each as thought-starters.

- *Church:* attendance, baptism, membership, serving in, giving to, learning in, praying with, fellowship, Lord's Supper, promoting unity
- *Discipleship:* meditation on Scripture, prayer, evangelism, missions, priorities/stewardship of time, fasting, silence and solitude, journaling, learning/reading, legalism vs. consistency
- *Family:* marriage, family crisis, unconverted family members, childlessness, dealing with aging parents, parenting children, parenting teenagers, divorce, sex, family devotions
- *Money:* giving, saving, investing, controlling debt, contentment, budgeting, gambling, wasting, not loving it, simplifying with less
- *Work:* purpose, amount of, travel, attitude toward, dependability, integrity, witness at, relationships (with boss, coworkers, customers, suppliers), integration of faith with, retirement

Train yourself to ask "How does the Bible speak to this?" To do this is a manifestation of love for God and love for His will. This is to see wisdom and sweetness in the ways of God. God made us to be governed by His Spirit through His Word. Let us learn to find His glory and our joy by living in accordance with His loving design.

CHAPTER THREE

THE MORE A PERSON LOVES, THE CLOSER HE
APPROACHES THE IMAGE OF GOD.
— MARTIN LUTHER

ARE YOU
MORE LOVING?

LET ME GET RIGHT TO THE POINT. JESUS SAID THAT LOVE IS THE
clearest mark of a Christian. "A new commandment I give to you,"
He announced in John 13:34-35, "that you love one another; as I
have loved you, that you also love one another. By this all will
know that you are My disciples, if you have love for one another."
If you are growing in your love for others—especially in your love
for Christians—then you are growing as a Christian.

Notice in God's Word the importance He places on love by
Christians (emphasis added):

- "This is My commandment, that you *love one another* as
  I have loved you." (John 15:12)
- "These things I command you, that you *love one
  another.*" (John 15:17)
- *Be kindly affectionate to one another with brotherly love.*
  (Romans 12:10)

- Owe no one anything except to *love one another,* for he who loves another has fulfilled the law. (Romans 13:8)
- *Let all that you do be done with love.* (1 Corinthians 16:14)
- For all the law is fulfilled in one word, even in this: *"You shall love your neighbor as yourself."* (Galatians 5:14)
- And *walk in love,* as Christ also has loved us and given Himself for us. (Ephesians 5:2)
- But concerning brotherly love you have no need that I should write to you, for you yourselves are taught by God to *love one another.* (1 Thessalonians 4:9)
- And let us consider one another in order to *stir up love* and good works. (Hebrews 10:24)
- *Let brotherly love continue.* (Hebrews 13:1)
- If you really fulfill the royal law according to the Scripture, *"You shall love your neighbor as yourself,"* you do well. (James 2:8)
- Since you have purified your souls in obeying the truth through the Spirit in sincere love of the brethren, *love one another fervently* with a pure heart. (1 Peter 1:22)
- And above all things *have fervent love for one another.* (1 Peter 4:8)
- For this is the message that you heard from the beginning, that we should *love one another.* (1 John 3:11)
- And this is His commandment: that we should believe on the name of His Son Jesus Christ and *love one another*, as He gave us commandment. (1 John 3:23)
- And this commandment we have from Him: that he who loves God must *love his brother also.* (1 John 4:21)
- And now I plead with you, . . . not as though I wrote a new commandment to you, but that which we have had from the beginning: that we *love one another.* (2 John 5)

Love is the badge and character of Christianity. A Christian may advance in many areas, including the ability to witness, teach, or even preach ("Though I speak with the tongues of men and of angels"), or biblical insight and knowledge ("And though I . . . understand all mysteries and all knowledge"), or faith, service, and giving ("and though I have all faith, . . . and though I bestow all my goods to feed the poor, and though I give my body to be burned"), but these mean little ("I have become sounding brass or a clanging cymbal. . . . I am nothing. . . . It profits me nothing") without growth in the most important Christian distinctive—love (1 Corinthians 13:1-3).

THE DECLINE OF LOVE

When love grows colder, our sin increasingly manifests itself and we look more *un*like Jesus. We lose patience easily, whereas 1 Corinthians 13:4 says that "Love suffers long." Unkindness becomes common, yet love "is kind." We become sinfully envious of the advantages and privileges of others, perhaps even of those within our own family; conversely, "love does not envy." When challenged about our lack of love, we quickly and quite confidently list all the sacrifices and other proofs of our love, and yet "love does not parade itself, is not puffed up." As our hearts harden against love, we become less courteous, especially to those closest to us, in contrast to love which "does not behave rudely" (1 Corinthians 13:5). We begin to consider ourselves and our "rights" as more important than others and their needs, whereas love "does not seek its own." When love is in decline we are more easily angered, but love "is not provoked." A lack of love is often faultfinding, and it mentally keeps score of offenses, but love "thinks no evil."

We're not growing in love when we have time for projects but not for people. Love is on the downgrade when it fails to protect, whether it's the reputation of friends or coworkers, or the physical *and* spiritual health of family members. Love has cooled when it is unwilling to confront when necessary. In the church this may manifest itself by a lack of support for biblical church discipline. You do not love others if you will let them ruin their lives, their testimony, their reputation, and bring shame upon the church and the name of Christ, and you are unwilling to try to rescue them according to God's plan (see Matthew 18:15-20 and 1 Corinthians 5) from the sin that has deceived them.

Love's decline may also be typified by unconcern for the lost. We become less sensitive to the physical needs of people and less burdened by others' spiritual needs. A declining love acts but is not "without hypocrisy" (Romans 12:9). Love's decline is not "given to hospitality" (verse 13). It is too indifferent to "rejoice with those who rejoice, and weep with those who weep" (verse 15). Perhaps worst of all, it is apathetic about the rise of things in the heart and life that are *contrary* to love.

The only person who loved without fail was Jesus Christ. Neither the apostle Paul, nor the apostle John, nor your favorite hero from Christian history always lived by the 1 Corinthians 13 standard of love. Scottish pastor Maurice Roberts observed that when it comes to growing in love, "The best believers find their progress slow and their attainments meager."[1] The point, however, is not speed, but direction. Are you making convincing progress in love, however slow, or are you regressing?

WHAT KIND OF LOVE?

Some people flatter themselves about how loving they are. They know that nothing means more to them than their children. Holidays are always spent with family. They consider themselves good neighbors and devoted friends. As their family and circle of friends grow, their love grows with it, right?

The Bible alone, and not our own hearts (which the Bible

depicts in Jeremiah 17:9 as "deceitful above all things, and desperately wicked") should be our standard both to define love and to describe it in practice. Too often we wrongly classify as love what the *King James Version* of the Bible calls "natural affection" (see Romans 1:31 and 2 Timothy 3:3). In normal circumstances, parents love their children, family members love each other, and people love their friends. This is true for Christians and nonChristians alike. God made us in such a way that, even in a fallen world, we naturally love certain people, thus the term *natural* affection.

Many people, therefore, are congratulating themselves for what amounts to merely being human, and they conclude amiss that this innate love testifies of spiritual health. Natural affection, however, is just one of several pretenders to the kind of love only those indwelt by the Holy Spirit can express. In his eighteenth-century masterpiece *Religious Affections,* Jonathan Edwards warned of these imitations, referring first to true Christian love:

> 'Tis the chief of the graces of God's Spirit, and the life,
> essence and sum of all true religion; and that by
> which we are most conformed to Heaven, and most
> contrary to hell and the devil. But yet it is ill arguing
> from hence, that there are no counterfeits of it. It may
> be observed, that the more excellent anything is, the
> more will be the counterfeits of it.[2]

Besides natural affection, there is another counterfeit love. Its loving actions are only a veneer for too much self-love. Any benefits it brings to others are secondary to the question, "Does it please me first?" A man will be absolutely convinced that he loves a beautiful woman, and indeed will do almost anything for her. He adores her, thinks of her constantly, and wants nothing more than her. But the truth is, he loves her only for what she does to and for *him.* She excites, intrigues, and arouses him. He does want her to be happy, but in reality he wants her to find her happiness in bringing pleasure to him. And he continues to love her only to the degree that she continues to please him. He will do nothing for her willingly or without hypocrisy unless it brings pleasure for him to do it anyway. This kind of love is just as common in other relationships as romantic ones. With parents or children, siblings, neighbors, or friends, we can act in loving ways, but either heartlessly or only because it pleases us to do so. We do not measure our growth in Christlikeness by the vicissitudes of this kind of love.

A similar counterfeit is the "I'll love you if you'll love me" type of love. This kind of love doesn't originate from a commitment to love, nor from a desire to be like Christ, but simply dispenses love as *quid pro quo*. This is not Christian love, rather it is the epitome of worldly love. Jesus put it this way: "But if you love those who love you, what credit is that to you? For even sinners love those who love them" (Luke 6:32). Edwards portrayed those who love like this:

> They are full of dear affections to some, and full of
> bitterness toward others. They are knit to their own
> party, them that approve of them, love them and
> admire them; but are fierce against those that oppose
> and dislike them. Some show a great affection for
> their neighbors, . . . the children of God abroad; and
> at the same time are uncomfortable and churlish
> towards their wives and other near relations at home,
> and are very negligent of relative duties.[3]

Can anyone think he is growing in love and thus becoming more like Jesus when, just like those who hated Jesus, he only loves with a reciprocal love? The test of Christlikeness is not the greatness of your love toward those who love you, but the bounty of your love toward those who do not.

Then there is the counterfeit of unbalanced love. It fails to treat people as a unity of body and soul, with both elements having legitimate needs. Again, Edwards exposes the error in this love:

> Some men show a love to others as to their outward man, they are liberal of their worldly substance, and often give to the poor; but have no love to, or concern for the souls of men. Others pretend a great love to men's souls, [but] are not compassionate and charitable towards their bodies. The making of a great show of love, pity, and distress for souls, costs 'em nothing; but in order to show mercy to men's bodies, they must part with money out of their pockets. But a true Christian herein is like the love and compassion of Jesus Christ. He showed mercy to men's souls, by laboring for them in preaching the gospel to them; and showed mercy to their bodies, in going about doing good, healing all manner of sickness and diseases among the people. We have a remarkable instance of Christ's having compassion at once both to men's souls and bodies, and showing compassion by feeding both, in Mark 6:34 etc.[4]

Jesus came primarily to save sinners forever, not merely to heal their short-lived bodies. His greatest display of love for us was in His death, for through it we experience the love of God unto eternal life. And the most loving thing we can ever do for anyone is give them the words that can lead to immortality in a radiantly glorious body. But "let us not love in word or in tongue, but in deed and in truth" (1 John 3:18). Those growing in Jesus' kind of love will not only say loving words but also do loving deeds, just as He did. (See chapter 5 for more on this subject of meeting both spiritual and practical needs.)

LOVE IN REAL LIFE

Those who are growing in love will demonstrate it in at least three areas. First, their *love for other Christians* will strengthen. One of the clearest indications that we have the Spirit of God is love for others in whom He lives: "We know that we have passed from death to life, because we love the brethren" (1 John 3:14). Relationships with Christian brothers and sisters in the church become indispensable to those who share eternal life. Like Christ, true Christians have a love for nonChristians, but they have a preferential love for those who love Christ. Just as we love many people, yet have a deeper love for those in our families, so we in God's family love one another more than we love those who hate Christ and His people. And as we are able, the Bible says that we should *express* our love by doing good to all people, but particularly those in our spiritual family: "Therefore as we have opportunity, let us do good to all, especially to those who are of the household of faith" (Galatians 6:10).

A second area of growth in love is *love for the lost.* A wealthy young man once came to Jesus and asked what he must do to inherit eternal life. The young man assumed he was in fairly good standing because he had tried to keep the Ten Commandments. But after he asserted this, "Jesus, looking at him," reports Mark 10:21, "*loved him,* and said to him, 'One thing you lack: Go your way, sell whatever you have and give to the poor, and you will have treasure in heaven; and come, take up the cross, and follow Me'" (emphasis added). In showing love to this man, Jesus did not compromise His message. He made it unmistakable that to have eternal life the man must forsake his god (that is, his possessions) and put Christ first. Although there is no indication that the man became Jesus' disciple, Jesus loved him nonetheless. The more we are like Jesus, the more we manifest the fruit of the Spirit and the more loving we will be to *everyone,* including those who are cold to the things of God. Jesus said we are even to love our enemies, and not just those who love us (Luke 6:27,32).

My wife, Caffy, has spent several hours recently doing home renovation for an unconverted couple we've come to love very much. She's doing it because she wants to love them toward Christ, that is, to show a sweaty love that might gain a hearing for the gospel. She has more than enough of her own work to do, but she is, to use Puritan Ralph Venning's term, "un-selfing" at this time because of her love for God, and the gospel, and her growing love for these people who, at present, are not interested in our message.

A third area to examine when measuring your growth in love is *love for your family*. For many who are reading these lines, this will be the most brutal part of the evaluation. Nowhere are we more aware of our unloving words and ways than at home. And yet, who we really are, we are at home. Even so, we must never believe that it is impossible to grow in love toward our family members. God does not derisively give us commands such as Ephesians 5:25: "Husbands, love your wives, just as Christ also loved the church and gave Himself for her." All Christians are meant to be growing Christians, and that includes observable growth in love for family members. Over time, those in your family—your spouse, your children, your parents, your siblings—should feel that you love them more than you used to. Maybe that will be expressed in more gratitude than previously, or less anger, or more physical affection, or more patience, responsibility, generosity, frugality, or simply by having more time for them.

In some areas, of course, an unbeliever could appear to be growing in love to a degree similar to that of a Christian. For example, if I had an unconverted neighbor who would rather watch a football game on TV, but he takes his daughter to the park instead, and I'd rather read, but I take my little girl to the park, why am I manifesting Christian love and my neighbor isn't? If a nonChristian and I do the same thing—namely, give up our own desires in order to willingly spend time with our children—why is my love "Christian" and his isn't? In both cases we show love because (1) our conscience tells us to do it, and (2) we're willing to put others before ourselves.

What's different for the Christian is that he also acts as he does because he believes what he's doing is the will of God. His love is more than self-sacrifice, for it contains a vertical God-ward dimension as well as a horizontal one. The awareness that you are doing something pleasing to God adds a quality and depth to love, as well as a satisfaction in the exercise of it, that the natural affection of the world cannot reproduce.

Moreover, the motive of Christian love at its best includes another facet that worldlings are incapable of knowing. Because "the love of God has been poured out in our hearts by the Holy Spirit who was given to us" (Romans 5:5), we are able to love out of the extravagant outpouring of God's love for us. An unbeliever can only pump love from his own limited, stagnant, brackish human reserves. The Christian, on the other hand, can pour out love from the love God pours in. He can show a love to others that effervesces from the fountain of his delight in knowing God. As John Piper put it, "Love is the overflow of joy in God which gladly meets the needs of others."[5] Jonathan Edwards adds, "It is love that arises from an apprehension of the wonderful riches of free grace and sovereignty of God's love to us in Christ Jesus."[6]

So, Christian, love begins with God. We love because He first loved us. Then the more satisfaction and delight we find in His love, the more we delight in loving others. The more enjoyment we find in God as God, the more we truly enjoy being like Him by loving others. The more we grow in our joy in God, the more joy we find in the joy others find in our loving actions.

CULTIVATING LOVE

Maurice Roberts asks,

> Why is real Christian love so scarce in the world? It is because its cultivation requires nothing less than the *reversal* of every instinct in our fallen natures. Love is against the grain of nature. It is against *every* fiber of our being as sinners. But nature, in the regenerate, is under the higher power of grace. . . . What the unregenerate cannot do, true Christians may and must.[7]

Whether this chapter has comforted you or confronted you, until you see Christ in Heaven you will always need to grow in love. Regardless of where you are now, here are some workable suggestions for maturing in the most Christlike of graces.

Meditate on love as the most important distinguishing mark of a Christian. In his article, "The Supreme Grace of Christian Love," Roberts wrote, "Love is the jewel among the graces of the Christian life. We know it—and perpetually forget it."[8] But don't just *remember* that love is the primary insignia of a Christian, *think* about it. I've known some Christians who, by the emphasis of their lives, stress knowledge or orthodoxy over love. While they would verbally assent to the priority of love, they almost seem to say as an excuse not to love, "But that's not my gift." Love is a gift from God, but not *that* kind of gift. Love is not the sort of spiritual gift like teaching or mercy (see the lists of gifts in Romans 12; 1 Corinthians 12; Ephesians 4) that we can say was given to some but not to us. Instead, the Bible insists, "He who does not love does not know God" (1 John 4:8). Do you give primacy to the pursuit of being more loving? If you want to grow in love, think about love. Review the Scriptures in the introductory section of this chapter to help in your meditation.

Let your heart be often warmed by the fire of God's love. God is the Source of the love that flames in the Christian heart.

We must bask in His love before we can expect it to consistently blaze forth from us toward others. This means, in part, that frequently in your times of prayer and meditation on Scripture you should let some aspect of God's love—especially the Cross—allure your attention like the mesmerizing flames in a fireplace. Pray much to "be able to comprehend with all the saints what is the width and length and depth and height—to know the love of Christ which passes knowledge" (Ephesians 3:18-19). "God is love," wrote an eminent Dutch minister of the late 1600s, "and having communion with God will cause us to grow warm in love."[9]

Discover assurance that God is your Father by loving as He loves. Because "love is of God," the inspired apostle John reasons, therefore "everyone who loves is born of God" (1 John 4:7). God's nature is love, and those who have His nature are His children. I recently saw a baby alligator. If I pointed to it and claimed, "That's my child," no one would take me seriously. Any child of mine would be born with a human nature, not that of an alligator. Anyone "born of God" will have His nature, that is, His loving nature. If you love to love others because you experience genuine joy at the joy prompted in others by your actions, take heart: those who show such love are the children of God.

Delight in imitating God. This is not a mystical platitude or a new ager's aspiration. The Bible speaks plainly about imitating God by showing love: "Therefore be imitators of God as dear children. And walk in love, as Christ also has loved us and given Himself for us" (Ephesians 5:1-2). To quote Roberts again, "Love, in its essence, is likeness to God."[10] Love people at times and in ways when you can thrill at the awareness, "I am being like God as I do this!"

Identify those relationships where you most need to grow in love. Does your family come to mind first? How about someone with whom you work? A neighbor? A person at church? Target

ARE YOU MORE LOVING?

specific people as you grow in love, not just everyone in general. In particular, *who* would know that your love is more Christlike, and *how* would they know? Once these faces are in your mind, . . .

Take the initiative in showing love, especially where you have little or no expectation of love in return. Let your delight in imitating God be enough, regardless of the response your loving initiatives receive. Isn't that what Jesus did? Aren't you reading this because you want to grow more like Him?

ARE YOU MORE SENSITIVE TO GOD'S PRESENCE?

WHEN WAS THE LAST TIME YOU THOUGHT, "GOD IS HERE"? PERHAPS it was during a time of unusually Spirit-anointed preaching of Holy Scripture. I recall a conference when the Lord seemed to be speaking so powerfully through the preacher of His Word that tears were coursing down my cheeks. I had been similarly moved before, but this time I didn't want to distract myself for even a couple of seconds to wipe the tears away lest I miss something from this experience with God.

Maybe you have felt God's presence in an extraordinary way during a time of passionate prayer with God's people. The Lord may have seemed so close that you were almost convinced that if you opened your eyes you would see Him.

Your Father may have been especially near in some experience in nature, as when reveling in the majestic grandeur of a Rocky Mountain vista or when awestruck while contemplating the sparkling immensity of the galaxy on a clear winter's night.

You may have perceived the nearness of the Holy One, as I have, while walking in solitude across a field or down a wooded path, hands in pockets, on a leisurely Lord's Day afternoon during leaf-turning season. Maybe you remember feeling enveloped in the presence of God in some placid place, a still moment at home without a single electronic hum anywhere and no grinding roar from any yard in the neighborhood. It could have been in the soundless serenity of a lakeside sunset when the coolness of the autumn evening carried you in reverie to the awareness of the presence of the Prince of Peace.

By contrast, you may have been thrust suddenly into a knowledge of God's closeness during an emotionally charged moment, as in a split-second, adrenaline-rushed deliverance from a car accident that appeared to be unavoidable. Or His presence may have been deeply felt in soft lamplight during tender gazes at the fingers and face of your sleeping newborn.

And surely you have known those moments in magnificent congregational worship when the Lord of glory seemed to be towering over the forest of exultant voices — those moments when God's presence is almost atmospheric.

But *how often* are you aware of the presence of God? If we take the teaching of the Bible seriously, perception of the presence of God should not be an occasional experience. I do not mean that we should frequently *feel* a supernatural presence, for that can be extremely unreliable. Nevertheless, it should not be unusual for us, wherever we are, to recognize that "God is here." As we grow closer to Him, generally speaking, we should discern His immanence more readily and more often.

"SURELY THE LORD IS IN THIS PLACE, AND I DID NOT KNOW IT"

Apparently, many professing Christians identify more with the words of Jacob "Surely the Lord is in this place, and I did not know it" (Genesis 28:16) than with the promise of Jesus when He said, "I am with you always" (Matthew 28:20). According to one survey, "Two out of every three adults (68 percent) who describe themselves as Protestant, Catholic or Christian say that *at some time* in their lives they felt as if they were in God's presence."[1] At some time? That means virtually nothing, for the same survey reveals that "more than half of all *non*Christians . . . (58 percent) also indicated that they felt they have been in His presence."[2] Furthermore, "among those who describe their church as being Protestant, Catholic or Christian, . . . one out of every eight (13 percent) has felt God's presence *one* or *two* times in their lives and 32 percent have *never* sensed His presence in their lives."[3] From those in the survey who openly described themselves as "born again Christians," the results were stunning: "one-third (32 percent) have either *never* felt God's presence or have sensed it *only once* or *twice* in their lives!"[4] (emphasis added).

What will result from a true Christian's dullness to God's company? For one thing, it necessarily means thinking less often of God, His Word, and His will. This is not a great deal different than an unbeliever who rarely thinks of God.

Insensitivity to the nearness of God certainly means less awareness that "the eyes of the LORD are in every place, keeping watch on the evil and the good" (Proverbs 15:3). That leads to thinking less of restraining sin on the one hand, or of doing good on the other. For after all, who will know? At such times we imitate Moses when "he looked this way and that way, and when he saw no one, he killed the Egyptian" (Exodus 2:12). No matter who we do *not* see, we must never forget the One whose presence is unseen yet more real than any other.

In effect, living apart from a conscious sense that the Lord

is present is to live as though God really is *not* there. More pleasure is sought in things, dreams, or people than in God. A relationship with God is reduced to mere religion. The spiritual
disciplines devolve into mere duty or even legalism. Public worship becomes an obligation, not a privilege. Obviously, this is not
the profile of a growing Christian.

HOW DO WE DISCERN GOD'S PRESENCE?

Before proceeding, we should understand there are several mean-
ings to the term "the presence of God." Theologians speak of:

- *The universal presence of God.* This is also called God's
  omnipresence, meaning that He is everywhere, and that
  there is no place where God is not. (See Psalm 139:5-12
  and Jeremiah 23:24.) That God is everywhere, however,
  does not mean that God is everything. Where there is a
  tree, God is an infinite Person who is everywhere that
  tree is, but the tree is not God.
- *The Christological presence of God.* God was and is present in Jesus Christ. See John 1:1,14 and Colossians 2:9.
  Jesus is Immanuel, "God with us" (Matthew 1:23).
- *The indwelling presence of God.* God is present by His
  Holy Spirit in a unique way within Christians. See John
  14:16-17. He is a second, distinct Person living with us
  in our bodies.
- *The perceptible presence of God.* God's presence is often
  perceived through His work or influence. See Luke 1:66
  and Acts 11:21. This is usually what is meant when we
  speak of someone, say, after a powerful sermon or personal witness, "The Lord was with him."
- *The heavenly presence of God.* God's presence is manifest
  in Heaven as in no other place. See Matthew 6:9 and
  18:10. It is the presence of God that makes it Heaven. His

glory and splendor are displayed there as nowhere else.

- *The eternal presence of God.* God's presence will either be forever enjoyed in Heaven or forever forfeited in hell. See Revelation 21:3 and 2 Thessalonians 1:9. However, because God is omnipresent, there is some sense in which He is even in hell. It is not the absence, but the presence of God in hell that is so terrifying and tormenting. He will be present, but manifesting only His divine wrath and justice, without His love and mercy.

All access to the presence of God, with His universal presence excepted, is through Jesus Christ. God the Son is the way to God the Father; no one comes to the Father except through Jesus (see John 14:6). "For there is one God," we are taught in 1 Timothy 2:5, "and one Mediator between God and men, the Man Christ Jesus." So when it comes to discerning the presence of God, one must first be "Immanuelized." That is to say, you can't reliably recognize the presence of "God with us" until you experience "Christ in you, the hope of glory" (Colossians 1:27). To know this indwelling presence of Christ, one must first, in Jesus' words, "Repent, and believe in the gospel" (Mark 1:15).

God's universal presence surrounds us as the air surrounds the soaring eagle or the Pacific engulfs the dolphin as it dives, "for in Him we live and move and have our being" (Acts 17:28). Even so, we could never discern the presence of God rightly and in truth if He did not first reveal Himself to us. He has revealed Himself generally to us through creation (Romans 1:20), but much more specifically through the Word. His self-revealing Word has come to us in two living ways: the incarnate Word (Jesus) and the written Word (the Bible). And it is through His Word that our experience with God, including our perception of His presence, is mediated.

What does this mean? It means that we don't try to experience the presence of God just any way that pleases us. I am concerned by current trends in evangelical spirituality toward mysticism, or what is sometimes called Christian mysticism. The essence of mysticism is the attempt to experience God unmediated, that is, without means. This is the belief that apart from any external assistance, you enter *directly* into an experience of the presence of God. Often this will be described as looking deep within your soul to meet the indwelling presence of God, or to imagine Him sitting with you. The problem is, as spiritual as this may sound, the Bible never commands us to do this or ever describes such an experience.[5]

Rather, what we are told to do is (1) seek Him through His Word, or (2) seek Him through experiences that are founded on His Word, or (3) seek Him through daily life in ways that are informed by His Word. In these ways, God is revealed and mediated to us through the gift He gave for that purpose: His Word.

As I read and meditate on Scripture, for example, or listen to it preached, I can expect to become aware that this is the voice of God I am hearing. As I participate in the ordained experiences of congregational worship and the Lord's Supper, by faith I can expect to find Christ's spiritual presence there. And when I'm walking in a forest or through the door to the place where I work, I can seek and sense the presence of God in such moments because the Bible informs me that God is there as well.

But this is different from the mystical way of just somehow "opening up" to the presence of God. A pagan or pantheist could do that. The difference for the Christian is that he can pursue and perceive the presence of God, not in an *immediate* (that is, unmediated) way, but mediated through truth that is revealed by God in the Bible. That's how a man or woman can walk into the workplace and say silently, "The Lord is here. I know that because God has said He is everywhere." And based upon that truth, he or she can affirm and enjoy the presence of God there.

When we seek the presence of God mediated—directly or indirectly—through Scripture, we are not imagining God as we would like Him to be. The basis of our experience with God is God-revealed truth, not our individual, idiosyncratic opinions about God. We are then much more likely to sense the presence of God as He really is rather than as a God comprised of our preferences. (And, incidentally, we are less likely to spout the motto of those who have made God into what they want Him to be: "*My* God isn't like that!")

At the moment, I am sitting in a porch swing, looking at green leafy trees with the late-August afternoon sun on them. The air is still. The summer evening insect noises have just begun. A blackbird *skreees* seventy-five yards to my right, hidden in a row of trees behind my neighbor's yard. Two houses down a teenager's radio is playing indistinctly. Far away is the drone of a lawnmower. God is here. Do I know that because I can feel Him? No, a nonChristian neighbor also could have a "spiritual experience" and call the experience, which is very real, something *other* than a sense of the presence of God. But I *know* God is here and I can enjoy His presence. How do I know? The Bible tells me so. I base my experience with God upon the Word of God.

But my experience with God must go beyond just knowing He is present, closer than my own breath, nearer than my own skin. The Bible also tells me of the *character* of the God who is present. So I know that I am to seek to experience a God who is not merely present, but holy. And I know that He is merciful and patient and enjoys having me talk with Him. I know there is One keeping company with me who knows everything about me at this (and every) moment—my thoughts, my motives, my fears, my aspirations, my emotions, my anxieties, my mental and physical condition—and who loves me beyond my comprehension. I know that the One whose presence surrounds me as the universe surrounds the earth has all power and is bringing all the world to His appointed conclusion. I perceive the presence of the One who has been an earthbound man like me and understands me thoroughly, and before whom I will stand in judgment. I engage the One who gave His life—from His first breath in Bethlehem to His last heartbeat on Calvary—to atone for my sins and who rose again to bring me to His heavenly home.

This is very different from seeking the presence of a virtually unknown god, a god about whom nothing is clear, distinct, or known. That would lead me to seek an experience rather than a Person, or else not be able to distinguish a Person from a presence. Without a mediated sense of God's presence, how can I know I have indeed encountered the God of the Bible? How can I be sure that I haven't delved into the recesses of a mysterious, imaginative mind and simply manufactured an experience? How do I even reassure myself (and others) that I have not in fact encountered a demonic presence masterfully masquerading as an "angel of light" (2 Corinthians 11:14)?

In his classic book on devotion to God, *The Knowledge of the Holy*, A. W. Tozer wrote of the person who apprehends the presence of God in the correct manner. To this one

> "the practice of the presence of God" consists not of
> projecting an imaginary object from within his own
> mind and then seeking to realize its presence; it is
> rather to recognize the real presence of the One
> whom all sound theology declares to be already there,
> an objective entity, existing apart from any apprehension of Him on the part of His creatures. The resultant
> experience is not visionary but real.[6]

So when I ask if you are more sensitive to God's presence than ever before, I'm not asking if you have had mystical experiences with an atmospheric sense of the Lord's nearness. Rather I'm inquiring whether you have increasingly paused to recognize the Lord's presence where you are and to consider who it is who is present, based upon His self-revelation. Have you been feasting on the sweetness of His presence, adoring the beauty of His presence, by delighting your mind in the revealed attributes of the omnipresent Lord?

GROWING THROUGH GOD'S DESERTIONS

I do not want to imply that to be growing spiritually means you must consistently increase your awareness of the presence of God. You can be growing when you least sense intimacy with the Lord.

In the first place, I doubt that any Christian grows more aware of God's presence every day and steadily for the rest of his life. That denies the realities of living as a sinner in a fallen world. Second, it is common for believers to have many seasons where, for their own spiritual good, God actually withdraws a conscious sense of His presence. The Puritans referred to such occasions as "God's desertions," times when we feel as though God has forgotten and forsaken us.[7] But even though God's presence is not perceived, He is no less near.

In *Pilgrim's Progress,* John Bunyan's timeless allegory on the spiritual life, the main character, Christian, travels through a dark and terrifying place called the Valley of the Shadow of Death. It is described as the worst trial through which he had yet come, and he had never felt so alone. Not only did the voice of God seem silent, but Christian also was so perplexed that "he did not know his own voice" from the blasphemies whispered to him by his spiritual enemy. "Sometimes," wrote Bunyan, "he had half a thought to go back; then again he thought he might be halfway through the Valley: . . . and that the danger of going back might be much more than for to go forward; so he resolved to go on."[8] And though Christian felt completely on his own, he was not. Pressing forward by faith alone he grew in ways he did not comprehend at the time.

If, while reading this chapter, you have thought, "I haven't been sensing God's presence much lately," take note that it's one thing to long for a sense of God's presence while not experiencing it, and another to live routinely with no awareness of His absence. There is a world of difference between Jesus crying out from the cross, "My God, My God, why have You forsaken Me?" (Matthew 27:46), and Samson saying just before his capture, "'I will go out as before, at other times,' . . . but he did not know that the LORD had departed from him" (Judges 16:20). One is known by its agony, the other by its apathy. Though you may be progressing in Christlikeness and persevering in the will of God, yet all along unaware that God is with you, take care that you do not become Samsonlike, content with or conditioned to life apart from a sense of His blessing.

John Stevenson, a British minister of the first half of the 1800s, urged the cultivation of this desire:

> The greatest of all spiritual and eternal blessings is the presence of God. On this our hearts' strongest desires ought to be fixed. This is the subject which warrants, and rewards, the most vehement importunity. Even in the greatest darkness of soul, even while the countenance of God is withdrawn, nothing can honor God more as a Creator, or gratify his heart more as a parent, than that we should make the light of his countenance the first and last object of our desires, and be restless and unhappy so long as it is turned away from us. Indeed, not to be importunate after this, proves that we are destitute of the feelings of a child, and shows that we possess little or no love to our Heavenly Father. It was this that well nigh burst the filial heart of Christ in the garden and on the Cross. His whole soul desired to enjoy the smile of his Father's countenance. He knew the goodness of his Father and he knew that the further he pressed into it the more of it he should obtain.[9]

OPENING YOUR SPIRITUAL EYES
TO HIS PRESENCE

What practical steps can we take to grow in our awareness of the continuous presence of God?

Go often to the place where God has revealed Himself most clearly—the Bible. Arguably Britain's most influential twentieth-century preacher, Martyn Lloyd-Jones said of God's Word, "The more we know it and read it, the more it will take us into the presence of God. So if you want to set the Lord always before you, spend much of your time with regular daily reading of the Bible."[10]

As obvious as this may seem at first, many who would purse their lips and nod their heads at these words would turn around and unwittingly put priority on seeking the presence of God in experiences where Scripture plays no role. Shouldn't we expect to experience God's presence *primarily* by means of that which He gave explicitly for the purpose of making Himself known to us: *His Word?*

But don't simply read from the Bible, close it, then walk away. Absorb the water of the Word of God through meditation. Otherwise, what you have read may be like rain that evaporates on a sidewalk. Linger over something from it so that it percolates into the soil of your soul. Listen long enough until you hear it for what it is—the voice of God.

Acknowledge His presence with you by talking with Him. Many wives complain that their husbands can sit in the same room with them for extended periods of time and never acknowledge their presence by speaking. Does this develop intimacy? Obviously not. When a person's prayer life is decaying by silence, is it any wonder that he or she feels unaware of the nearness of God? God is a real Person who is very present. Ignore Him and He will seem distant. Talk with Him and you will almost always feel Him closer.

As I mentioned in chapter 1, I want to commend now in this

context the practice of praying through a passage of Scripture, especially one of the Psalms. Let the words that have originated in the heart and mind of God Himself become the vehicle to carry the burdens of your heart and mind back to God. I've taught this ancient way of prayer in seminars from California to the Carolinas, and countless people have testified that praying from God's Word brings them into the presence of God as never before. Praying this way makes prayer more what it ought to be, namely, a real conversation with a real Person.

Seek Him in the manifestations of His presence given only in congregational worship. The Bible says that the body of each Christian is a temple of the Holy Spirit (1 Corinthians 6:19). But specific references to being a temple of the Holy Spirit are made far more often about the *congregation* of believers than about individual believers (for example, see 1 Corinthians 3:9,16-17). So there is a sense in which going to worship with the people of God is going to the Lord's temple where His presence abides. In a true church, His Word is preached, His Son is presented in the Lord's Supper, His Spirit ministers through many and diverse gifts, and so forth. The solitary worshiper does not have access to the presence of the Lord in exactly these ways. While there are experiences with God that are given only in private worship, it is equally true that the Lord manifests His presence in ways unique to public worship.

Continually reaffirm the truth that He is omnipresent. The truth is, God is everywhere at all times. Immanuel Himself specifically promised His people, "I am with you always" (Matthew 28:20). The Lord is with us even when we don't sense His presence. We must, however, reaffirm what we know to be true, even when we don't feel it to be true. This will help us to live more by faith than by feelings.

"God seems so far away," my strongest feelings may say to me. "Doesn't He see what's happening? Why doesn't He answer my prayers?"

Faith in the truth responds, "But God *is* here. He promised He would never leave me or forsake me. Whether I sense His presence or not, the truth is: God is here with me as much as at any moment in my life. I will believe the *truth*."

Reaffirming the truth will also prompt us to look more for evidence of the presence of God around us. The great fourth-century Christian leader Augustine is said to have been confronted one day by a man who brandished his idol and demanded, "Here is my god, where is yours?" Augustine replied, "I cannot show you my God; not because there is no God to show, but because you have no eyes to see Him."

Unlike Augustine's opponent, Christians have been given the Holy Spirit, who enlightens us to see and believe the revelation of God in creation, in Christ, and in Scripture—in ways the natural man cannot (1 Corinthians 2:9-16). However, the fact that we have eyes to see does not mean we use them to look where we ought. In other words, there is often much more evidence of the presence of God around us than we appreciate.

Take a look around for a moment and notice everything in your sight that is blue. Go ahead. When you do, you develop "blue eyes," that is, eyes sensitive to the things around you that are blue. We need to develop "God eyes." We need to develop the sensitivity to see evidence of what we know to be true, namely, that God is with us. Look for God everywhere and in everything. Say to yourself often, "The Lord is here," especially in the ordinary places of life. While sitting at the computer, or when at the gas pump, the mall, or the grocery store, remind yourself that the Lord is present. Whether you are in the car, the kitchen, or involved in the most earthy and intimate experiences of life, reaffirm the fact that God is with you.

As we develop these "God eyes," we will be more like Jesus, who always recognized His Father's presence. Spurgeon says of Him:

He fed the multitude, but it was with his Father's bread; and he healed the sick, but the Father did the works. . . . Other men remarked that the ravens were fed, but he said, "Your Heavenly Father feeds them." Other men noticed the lilies were fair to look upon, but he discerned that "God so clothes the grass of the field." The Heavenly Father was in every place, and in every thing to Jesus. . . . Refuse to see anything without seeing God in it.[11]

Let me close by addressing those who regularly find themselves in situations or places that seem totally void of God. Reaffirm your faith that the Lord *is* there, and ask Him to remind you the next time you are in that place or set of circumstances. Think of one object, sound, or activity that occurs in each of these situations and let it be a reminder to pray, "Lord, I do believe that You are here and I thank You for Your presence."

Regardless of how sensitive you are to the presence of God at this point in your Christian pilgrimage, the prayer of A. W. Tozer is an appropriate way to end this chapter and to begin growing onward:

Our Father, we know that Thou art present with us, but our knowledge is but a figure and shadow of truth, and has little of the spiritual savor and inward sweetness such knowledge should afford. This is for us a great loss and the cause of much weakness of heart. Help us to make at once such amendment of life as is necessary before we can experience the true meaning of the words, "In thy presence is fullness of joy." Amen.[12]

CHAPTER FIVE

THERE IS NOTHING IN WHICH MEN RESEMBLE GOD
MORE TRULY THAN IN DOING GOOD TO OTHERS.
—JOHN CALVIN

DO YOU HAVE A GROWING CONCERN FOR THE SPIRITUAL AND TEMPORAL NEEDS OF OTHERS?

ABOUT ONE HUNDRED YEARS AFTER THE DEATH AND RESURRECTION of Jesus Christ, Antoninus Pius ruled the Roman Empire. Because everyone in those days was required to worship the emperor, Christians were considered disloyal and were under constant attack as followers of an illegal religion. They weren't officially persecuted by Antoninus Pius, but they had to defend themselves incessantly against false accusations. Just as we read in the book of Acts about how Paul was often hated by those who didn't know him and that riots sometimes broke out when lives were changed by his ministry, so it was with Christians in the decades after Paul's labors. Christians were continually deflecting the false charges and undeserved blame being hurled at them.

On one of these occasions, a famous Grecian philosopher from Athens named Aristides—who had himself become a Christian—was called upon to make a defense of the Christians before Antoninus Pius. Part of his defense was this: "They love one another. The widow's needs are not ignored, and they rescue the orphan from the person who does him violence. He who has gives to him who has not, ungrudgingly and without boasting."[1]

Christianity is a religion of concern for others. Among what are called the "great religions of the world," Christianity has no parallel when it comes to demonstrating concern for people and for their needs. Whether the needs are temporal or eternal, felt or unperceived, no other religion is known for its love and compassion, not only for those within its ranks, but particularly toward those outside its circle of adherents.

The perceptive eye and the helping hand are birthmarks of the born again in Christ. Concern for others is as much a part of being a Christian as concern for self is for the nonChristian. Meeting needs is the way of Jesus. And those following Jesus can trace their progress toward His likeness by tracking their growth in their concern for the spiritual and temporal needs of others.

THE BIBLICAL NEAR-BALANCE

The Bible clearly teaches Christians to be concerned for both the spiritual and the temporal needs of people. Jesus, our Lord and example, often demonstrated this dual concern by healing bodies and teaching truth on the same occasion. This twofold emphasis on both preaching and meeting temporal needs characterized the church immediately after Pentecost: "And with great power the apostles gave witness to the resurrection of the Lord Jesus. And great grace was upon them all. Nor was there anyone among them who lacked; for all who were possessors of lands or houses sold them, and brought the proceeds of the things that were sold" (Acts 4:33-34). When the apostles James,

Peter, and John agreed that Paul and Barnabas should go as missionaries to the Gentiles, Paul reports that in addition to sending them as preachers, "They [James, Peter, and John] desired only that we should remember the poor, the very thing which I also was eager to do" (Galatians 2:10).

Evangelicals as a whole typically tend to put more time, money, and prayer into labors of missions and evangelism than in social ministries. While I believe this approach as a rule is biblically sound, we must be alert to the danger inherent in our emphasis, namely, overlooking temporal needs. For instance, James 2:15-16 asks the question, "If a brother or sister is naked and destitute of daily food, and one of you says to them, 'Depart in peace, be warmed and filled,' but you do not give them the things which are needed for the body, what does it profit?" In other words, giving a spiritual blessing (such as sharing the gospel) without meeting an urgent physical need profits no one, especially the one on the receiving end. Evangelism that ignores hollow-eyed hunger or other crying needs of the ones being evangelized is a physical contradiction to the spiritual message. To say in effect, "I love you so much and am so concerned about you that I want to give you the words of eternal life, but I don't care enough to address your basic and pressing physical need," is a denial of my supposed concern.

Even so, I rarely see such self-contradictory evangelism. Others, though, claim it is a common failure by those who believe in the necessity of the new birth. No doubt it happens, but those who swing this accusation as a club the most are often the same ones who feed the body and starve the eternal soul. They demonstrate great concern for the physical or material needs but seldom get around to sharing the gospel. Their strategy implies that the *example* of Christlike actions will somehow feed the more important spiritual need. This method is at least as deadly as the opposite error of giving only Bible verses or gospel tracts to those who have desperate temporal needs.

Humility requires us to realize that whenever the Bible presents complementary truths like these, we all tend to lean one way or the other. Take Jesus' command "God is Spirit, and those who worship Him must worship in spirit and truth" (John 4:24) as a case in point. He calls for true worship to be done both in spirit *and* truth, but most of us feel a little more at home in worship with an emphasis on spirit *or* truth. (The same unbalanced tendency is as true for churches as it is for individual Christians.) Chances are you're like me in that you are more comfortable with sharing the gospel *or* feeding the hungry, answering questions about the Bible *or* driving nails on a widow's roof, bringing comfort from Scripture *or* bringing clothes to the needy. But as we grow more like Jesus, we will see ministry to temporal needs not as competing with, but as complementing, the meeting of spiritual needs.

JESUS THE NEED-MEETER

Jesus Christ, the ultimate need-meeter, reflected the "near-balance" of filling spiritual as well as temporal needs. He laid aside His heavenly privileges and came to earth for the expressed purpose of meeting our greatest need. As He put it, "I have come that they may have life" (John 10:10).

The supreme need of every human is a spiritual one. Because we have all willingly sinned by breaking the laws of God (Romans 3:23) and have done so an infinite number of times, we face physical death (Romans 6:23), judgment (Hebrews 9:27), and the second death of eternal punishment (Revelation 21:8). But "Christ was offered once to bear the sins of many" (Hebrews 9:28). He came to provide the only hope of escape "from the wrath to come" (1 Thessalonians 1:10). Jesus said of Himself, "I am the door. If anyone enters by Me, he will be saved" (John 10:9). To all who do come to Him in repentance and faith (Mark 1:15) Jesus promised, "I give them eternal life" (John 10:28). Jesus Christ came to offer Himself as the door to life in the next world—an incomprehensibly glorious and joyous life without comparison or end. Life with God Himself.

While His primary purpose was to meet our eternal need, He was not oblivious to people's temporal needs. His method of accomplishing both aims is perfectly demonstrated in the account recorded in Mark 6:34-44. "And Jesus, when He came out, saw a great multitude and was moved with compassion for them, because they were like sheep not having a shepherd. So He began to teach them many things" (verse 34). His compassion for their hopelessness prompted Him to teach them truth from Heaven. Then, after feeding their souls, He fed their hungry stomachs in what is known as the miracle of the feeding of the five thousand.

If we saw people from Jesus' perspective, we would begin to see them as "sheep not having a shepherd." Even though many do not feel themselves to be in such a condition, they are. Even if they appear to have no temporal needs, they certainly have spiritual needs. They may appear as self-sufficient as the hardened atheist Madalyn Murray O'Hair once did. But deep within they are often like her when she wrote at least a half-dozen times in her diary the plea, "Somebody, somewhere, love me."[2] Everyone is needy, no matter how thick his or her veneer of self-sufficiency. The one universal common denominator is that everyone has spiritual needs, chief of which is the need for Jesus, the soul-shepherd.

No one who is indwelled by the Spirit of Jesus can remain unfeeling toward either the temporal or the spiritual needs of others made plain. Growth in Christlikeness involves perceiving those needs *sooner* than before, and not just when they become obvious to everyone. Increased growth in Christian maturity is revealed by a heartfelt compassion toward people, not a perfunctory, merely external response. There is no Christlikeness in throwing money at a physical need or in dutifully reading a few Bible verses to an unbeliever and apathetically sending him on his way to hell.

This is not to say that the existence of a need always equals the call to meet it. Not even Jesus responded to every need He could have met. It's true, there were occasions when He "healed all who were sick" (Matthew 8:16), but this wasn't always the case. The Gospels tell us there were many times, such as the one recorded in Luke 12:1, "when an innumerable multitude of people had gathered together, so that they trampled one another." Jesus frequently had thousands pressing around Him—all with their needs—and many of them screaming for just His touch on a dying spouse or child, pleading with Him for healing or sight, begging Him to have mercy. Yet sometimes He walked on or sailed away. But even when He did this, He was conscious of the needs. And He turned away only because He was turning *to* something else He knew to be the will of God for Him at that moment. Sometimes the growing Christian must do the same.

THE HEROES OF CHRISTIAN HISTORY

The men and women who are most admired by the church have always been those disciples of Jesus most like Him in showing love by meeting both the spiritual and temporal needs of people.

In just one of many possible fields to consider, notice how many Christians known for devotion and zeal have also been committed to the care of children and orphans. As far back as the fifth and sixth centuries, it was Christian influence that brought legal protection to the children of the Roman Empire. After the Swiss reformer Huldreich (Ulrich) Zwingli (1484–1531)—a contemporary of Luther and Calvin—broke with the Roman church, he persuaded the Council of Zürich to transform several local monasteries into orphanages.

One of the most fruitful evangelists in history, George Whitefield (1714–1770) devoted much of his income to the development of an orphanage in colonial Georgia. Think of the impact upon tens of thousands of children accomplished by the devout William Wilberforce (1759–1833), who persevered for decades in the British Parliament to begin the modern movement to end slavery. At the same time, English missionary William Carey (1761–1834) was responsible for outlawing the centuries-old practices of child sacrifice and widow burning in India. Later in the 1800s, a Christian statesman, Anthony Ashley Cooper (also known as Lord Shaftesbury) (1801–1883), led the fight against child labor practices and sought to improve treatment of the mentally ill in Great Britain.

George Müller (1805–1898) is high among the church's great champions of prayer and faith, recording more than fifty thousand specific answers to prayer in his journals. Most of these prayers, however, were for the same purpose, namely, that God would be glorified by providing the means to feed, clothe, house, and educate up to two thousand orphans at a time in nineteenth-century Bristol, England. The Lord was pleased to channel tens of millions of dollars through Müller's hands, though he never made his needs known to anyone but God.

It is often unrecognized that Charles Haddon Spurgeon (1834–1892), remembered primarily as the Prince of Preachers, built more than seventeen homes for elderly widows and an orphanage for hundreds of children of all races and backgrounds, and eventually started and/or presided over *sixty-six* ministry organizations. Most of these served in the poorer parts of London, and on occasion were funded entirely by Spurgeon himself.

Today in America, Christians in every state of the Union provide homes and education for children without parents and for unwed expectant mothers. Moreover, the followers of Jesus are the ones spearheading the effort to protect the lives of the unborn.

Throughout history, Christians have led the way in supporting widows and orphans, building hospitals, and providing disaster relief on every continent in the world. Wherever a beachhead for the gospel of Jesus Christ has been established, medicine, education, and relief for the poor have followed.

Whether the need is hunger, lack of drinking water, illiteracy, sickness, homelessness, or anything else that causes misery, Christians have been at the forefront of caring for the needs of the world.

Christianity is a religion of concern for others.

But the greatest demonstration of Christlike concern has been the effort to obey the Great Commission of Jesus and take the good news about Him to everyone in the world. Growing Christians remember that the foremost need of anyone, anywhere, anytime is salvation, to be made right with God. This was preeminent on the heart of Jesus. As we become more like Him, we'll discover that the burden on His heart is weighing heavier on ours also.

GROWING FROM HERE

Too out of balance? Have you been saying the right things, but doing nothing to meet the spiritual or temporal needs of others? What now?

Go to the Great Ophthalmologist. Jesus is often called the Great Physician. But He could also be known as the Great Ophthalmologist, or Doctor of the Eyes. During His earthly ministry He healed the blind primarily to show that His miraculous power can open the eyes of the *spiritually* blind. Our spiritual darkness is forever banished once we see "the light of the knowledge of the glory of God in the face of Jesus Christ" (2 Corinthians 4:6). If He has already given you spiritual sight, go to the Great Ophthalmologist now and ask Him to increase your sight to see more as He sees.

Last year I had eye surgery. After a five-minute laser procedure on each eye, my eyesight went from being in the worst 15 percent in America to a normal 20/20—but not immediately. Although the improvement was dramatic by the time the bandages were removed the next morning, months passed before my vision was fully corrected. I saw my ophthalmologist frequently, and under his care I came to see even better than I had with glasses.

Once we have been born again, "all things have become new" (2 Corinthians 5:17), including our spiritual vision. The Holy Spirit enlightens us to see so much in ourselves, in the Bible, and in the world that we never saw before. But our eyesight is not yet perfect. Keep going to the Great Ophthalmologist and asking Him to enable you to see the needs He wants you to meet.

As your vision becomes more Christlike, you'll begin to see temporal and spiritual needs of people that you didn't see before. You'll detect inward tears before they well in the eyes, and hollowness of heart in those who don't even themselves know how empty they are. Hurts and needs you had never noticed will begin to emerge from the most familiar people and places.

Does this describe your spiritual vision? If not, it's time for a checkup. Ask the Great Ophthalmologist to correct your spiritual myopia.

Look for the hurt in every heart and home. More than twenty years of pastoral ministry have taught me that there is a hurt in *every* heart and home. This is true even for the wealthy or those who appear most to "have it all together." I remember one particular couple I pastored for two years before I learned of their greatest hurt. I was quite close to them, for the husband was the leading layman in our church and his wife taught our women's Bible study. He was a top attorney at the international headquarters of one of the best-known corporations in the world. Despite all this earthly success and solid spiritual leadership, they carried—unknown to anyone in our church at the time—one of the heaviest burdens in our fellowship. One night, ten years earlier in another city, their teenage son experimented with drugs. This first and only occasion permanently altered his mental condition. Until then he had been a model son and student with the brightest of futures. After that night he was the source of overwhelming heartache. Because he no longer lived with his parents, no one in our church knew of the grief, the cost, and the difficulty that often dominated their private lives. Many in our church considered this couple prosperous and trouble-free, when in fact few would have exchanged circumstances with them.

I've read statistics showing that every household in the United States experiences a crisis or significant life change every six months on average. This includes events such as a birth, death, injury, serious illness, job change or transfer, car accident, financial reversal, or child leaving home. Each of these situations may result in new opportunities to meet spiritual and/or temporal needs with the love of Christ. While writing this chapter I was able to share the gospel with a friend who for three years has brushed off my attempts to talk about the things of God. But a few days after his father died, I walked over and found him quite willing to discuss eternal things and his own mortality.

Some readers can look up from this page and immediately see a world full of needs framed by their windows. You make eye contact daily with many who have acute needs for food, clothing, shelter, medical treatment, work, and the like. Others who are scanning these lines may spend their lives primarily in a world where most of the needs stay hidden, like internal bleeding. If you are in the latter group, try looking through "need filters," and the opportunities for Christlike ministry will become obvious.

Here's what I mean: look at your neighborhood, your workplace, your classes, your church, your family, with the filter of "What are his/her/their spiritual needs?" Then, "What are his/her/their temporal needs?" By looking with these filters on the eyes of your mind, you will see some needs in sharper focus. This increased perception is in itself a sign of spiritual growth. In some cases you will conclude there are needs that you, by God's grace and His Spirit, should attempt to meet.

Knowing there is a hurt in every heart and home, your filtered eyes may see pressing needs you had never seen before in relation to widows, the elderly, children, single parents, the lonely, the homebound, the disabled, the ill or infirm, or the international student. The Great Ophthalmologist may show you people who need yard or garden help, transportation, errands run, home or car repairs, cleaning, meals, computer help, snow removal, firewood, painting, roof work, gutter cleaning, childcare, or just an extra hand given in Jesus' name. Or He may help you see more clearly those who need the gospel, prayer, biblical counsel, encouragement, reproof, a listening ear, an invitation to church, discipleship, an audiotape, CD, article, book, or a simple "How-are-you-doing?" visit.

Do something for the gospel and the good of others. Would God have you see so many needs and meet none? He doesn't expect you to meet every need shown to you, for not even Jesus did that. But our fulfilling Father does expect us to find so much joy in Him that, like Jesus, we will find pleasure and satisfaction in meeting the needs of others for His sake.

Remember when Jesus washed His disciples' feet in John 13:1-17? We're told that "Jesus, knowing that the Father had given all things into His hands, and that He had come from God and was going to God, rose from supper," took a towel, and washed their feet (see verses 3-5). It was out of knowing the joy and glory He had when in Heaven with the Father, and the awareness of the pleasure and joy in God to whom He was returning, that He was willing to meet the needs of a dozen pairs of dirty feet. Find joy in God and you will find joy in doing the work of God.

Don't sit passively until you "feel led" to particular needs. Go adventurously into your world with the gospel and the love of Christ, and you'll find Him guiding you to the needs He wants you to meet. And as you become His instrument in meeting the needs of others, you'll find Him meeting many needs of your own.

CHAPTER SIX

THE CLOSER YOU ARE TO THE LORD, THE CLOSER YOU
WILL BE TO OTHER BELIEVERS.
—PETER JEFFREY

DO YOU DELIGHT IN THE BRIDE OF CHRIST?

AGUR, ONE OF THE ANCIENT WRITERS OF PROVERBS, ACKNOWLEDGED:

There are three things which are too wonderful for me,
Yes, four which I do not understand:
The way of an eagle in the air,
The way of a serpent on a rock,
The way of a ship in the midst of the sea,
And the way of a man with a virgin. (Proverbs 30:18-19)

I don't know much about eagles, serpents, and ships, but I
have observed (and experienced) that the ways of a man with
a woman he loves are indeed often full of wonder. In order to
fulfill the requirements mandated by Laban for his daughter's
hand in marriage, the Old Testament patriarch "Jacob served
seven years for Rachel, and they seemed only a few days to him

because of the love he had for her" (Genesis 29:20). Long years, even long distances, are irrelevant when a man delights in a woman. I was in a Texas seminary while engaged to Caffy. She was living in northwest Arkansas where we'd met while I attended law school. My delight in her made me more than willing to make the six-hour drive from Fort Worth to Fayetteville whenever possible.

On an infinitely grander scale, Jesus made an incomparable journey from Heaven and worked for more than thirty years for the delight of His eyes, the church. "Christ also loved the church," writes Paul, "and gave Himself for her, that He might sanctify and cleanse her with the washing of water by the word, that He might present her to Himself a glorious church, not having spot or wrinkle or any such thing, but that she should be holy and without blemish" (Ephesians 5:25-27).

Now suppose that the very Spirit of Jesus Christ Himself were given to dwell, not only in the body of Jesus, but also in another human. (And realize that according to the New Testament, this is what happens to all who belong to Christ—see Romans 8:9.) Obviously then, like Christ, the man or woman who has been given the Spirit of Jesus would love what Jesus loves and died for—His bride, the church. So one of the best tests of whether we belong to Christ is whether *we* delight in *His* delight, namely, the people who comprise His church. Or as the apostle John put it, "We know that we have passed from death to life, because we love the brethren" (1 John 3:14).

King David's Old Testament words are a beautiful description of this New Testament love that God's people have for each other:

As for the saints who are in the earth,
They are the majestic ones in whom is all my delight.
(Psalm 16:3, NASB)

Notice the word "saints" in the first half of the verse. In the Bible, "saints" is one of the terms applied to the people of God.

Paul refers to Christians as saints in nearly every New Testament letter he wrote, using the word more than fifty times. These first-century saints were ordinary Christians, but not nominal ones. They were sincere followers of Jesus, manifesting the fruit of the Spirit (see Galatians 5:22-23). Far from perfect though, some of those he called saints were struggling with scandalous sin problems, as with the saints in the church at Corinth (see 1 Corinthians 1:2). But what was true then is true now—everyone indwelled by the Spirit of God is a saint, or as the Greek word literally means, a "holy one." Saints aren't exceptionally devoted believers now in Heaven, rather they are people who believe and live the Word of God in their workaday world—the kind of people David spoke of as "saints who are *in the earth*" (emphasis added). Yet David's delight was in such folk. He sought them out and took pleasure in their company because they loved God too.

David even waxed rhapsodical over his fellow saints, calling them "majestic ones." Other translations render the Hebrew word here as "excellent ones" or "glorious ones." Do you ever refer to your fellow believers in such magnificent terms? When you think of John the computer programmer who teaches the teenagers in your church, or Mary the homemaker who works with the children, do you say to yourself, "There's a majestic one!"? Let me remind you that God Himself inspired Israel's king to use such a description of God's people. As children of *the* Majestic One in Heaven they were His "majestic ones" in the earth, changed by the power of God. So it wasn't because of their own majesty, excellence, or glory that David delighted in them; it was because they shared with him a love for the majesty, excellence, and glory of God above all else. They loved the true Majesty, and this made them, and only them, majestic ones in David's sight.

Delighting in *Christ's* people is normal, healthy *Christian*ity. So permit me to ask you this question to help you diagnose your spiritual health: Do *you* delight in the bride of Jesus Christ?

Do you take pleasure in those who bring pleasure to Him?

In one sense I'm asking if you delight in the church as a whole, not in each Christian in particular. After all, the bride of Christ is the church, not individual Christians. Jesus is not a polygamist. The "marriage supper of the Lamb" (Revelation 19:9) is an event with all Christians collectively, not with each believer individually. The truth of Scripture is better expressed by a congregation confessing, "We are the bride of Christ," than by a solitary Christian saying, "I am the bride of Christ." Therefore, do you delight in the church, that is, in the gathering of believers, their corporate experiences and labor?

And yet, although Jesus' joy is in one bride, she is made of millions of individual Christians with faces and names, including those of people where you live. It would be very strange to say that you love Christ's church but dislike the people in her. But the attitude of some toward the church and her members is like the character in a cartoon I once saw who smirked, "I love mankind; it's people I can't stand."

In short, delighting in "the saints who are in the earth" means finding irresistible joy in the presence and the ministry of Christ's people, both in their congregational form and as individuals. Does this describe you?

DO YOU DELIGHT IN HER WILLINGLY?

A Davidlike delight in "the saints who are in the earth" is a God-given delight poured into the soul from Heaven, not ground out from the grit of determination. It does not require setting the jaw and resolving, "I *will* delight in these people," but more of the spontaneous spirit of "I was *glad* when they said to me, 'Let us go into the house of the LORD'" (Psalm 122:1, emphasis added). When God makes a Christian, He changes the person's heart so dramatically that delighting in the followers of Jesus becomes as easy and natural for the soul as delighting in sunsets and savory food is for the senses.

Something is amiss when a person participates in the life of a church only because of the forces of "ought." Parental training, family expectations, long-term habits, the heavy weight of conscience, and a sense of duty are not the overriding compulsions of the Christlike as they arise on the Lord's Day to gather with God's own. That is not to say that rightly motivated worshipers have none of the other influences, for some of them are quite healthy. But the primary motivation for growing Christians is "want," not "ought."

Any true delight is always a willing delight, not a reluctant one. Delight in the people of God cannot be forced into the soul any more than parents can coerce their single adult son to delight in a potential mate who holds no attraction for him. Nor will anyone delight in the church primarily because we shame them for delighting in the NFL, a hobby, or something else more than the family of God. The church is not a taste to be acquired, a new preference developed by sheer resolve. Just as candy delights a child, so the child of God does not have to be persuaded to delight in the supernatural spiritual sweetness found only in God's church. Delight in the church is inborn in those who are born again.

DO YOU DELIGHT IN HER COMPANY?

Some things, simply by their nature, delight us with their company. How easy it is to delight in a baby who smiles at you over the shoulder of his or her mother. For the Christian, the presence of the "saints who are in the earth," just by virtue of their being saints, evokes delight. For what makes these people to be saints in the earth is the God in the heavens—the most delightful Being in the universe—living in them and working through them.

When authentic Christians assemble in a local church, the omnipresent God dwells in their midst in a special way. While it's true that individual Christians are called the temple of the Holy

Spirit (1 Corinthians 6:19), that kind of language is far more often spoken of believers collectively. In the following God-inspired words of the apostle Paul, each use of the word "you" is plural, referring to the entire church to whom the letter was written:

- You are the temple of God . . . the Spirit of God dwells in you. (1 Corinthians 3:16)
- For you are the temple of the living God. (2 Corinthians 6:16)
- You also are being built together into a dwelling of God in the Spirit. (Ephesians 2:22)

So the reason why growing Christians so readily delight in being with the saints of God is the real presence of God Himself living within ordinary people we know. Ultimately, you are delighted by Him in them.

This is why haters of God and church, once they come to know God through Jesus Christ, begin to show new affection for the things of God, including the people of God. As lovers of God, they become lovers of the living temples of God.

This doesn't mean that growing Christians experience spiritual elation in every encounter with fellow believers or that delighting in the church is a perfect or unmixed delight. God dwells in people who still sin, and sometimes we leave a gathering of Christians with more of the stench of sin in our nostrils than the sweet aroma of the presence of God. Occasionally our mortal bodies will sit in the worshiping congregation of saints feeling sick or exhausted, not exhilarated. At times the Christian company we keep can actually leave us bored. Overall, however, God's people, when they are with others of God's people, find their minds enlightened and their hearts warmed in ways they never do when with those who are not indwelled by the Fire of Heaven.

Recently, a group of fifteen or twenty believers I know had a meal together after church, then spent the afternoon around the tables in Christian fellowship. As they were about to leave, they decided, "Why not eat together again?" And so they did. Arriving just before 10 A.M. for worship, they didn't separate until 7 P.M. Why? Because as growing Christians do, they delighted in each other's company.

DO YOU DELIGHT IN HER ACTIVITY?

From the first days of his ministry until the end of his ministry decades later, the apostle Paul faced opposition and persecution in his work. Why did he willingly endure so many imprisonments, beatings, and stonings and for so long (see 2 Corinthians 11:23-28)? Near the end of his life, in the last of his letters included in Scripture, Paul gave the answer: "I endure all things for the sake of the elect" (2 Timothy 2:10). Like his master, Jesus, the old apostle found unequaled delight in his work on behalf of God's elect, the church.

God doesn't keep the world turning so that we can do more business, make more money, and buy more things. Rather, God keeps the planet in motion because He has not finished the work of the church, that is, building the kingdom of His Son. Because this is God's purpose, it ought to be ours as well. And if we'll see it for what it is, we will delight in it (just as God does).

In an episode of TV's *Star Trek: The Next Generation*, Captain Picard found himself near death and caught a glimpse of what his life might have been like had he made some less bold choices in his earlier years. He realized how easily he could have become "just a dreary man with a tedious job." Ultimately, however, anyone—from a starship captain on down—who lives with a this-life-only perspective is a dreary person with a tedious job because he lives and works for something that is perishing. The relatively small percentage of those who think they have exciting lives and stimulating jobs fail to see that, in light of eternity, they are trying to satisfy themselves with that which is merely temporal.

The work of Christ's church is the greatest, most soul-satisfying enterprise in the universe. Nothing compares—career, family, conquest, success, wealth, politics, retirement—nothing! Furthermore, it is the only eternally enduring work we can do. Those who aren't committed to the work of the church are not just extremely shortsighted and self-defeating, but they also forfeit an incredible privilege. To delight yourself in anything else more than in God and the work of His kingdom is like contenting yourself with watching a video of someone else's wedding ceremony when you could be on your honeymoon.

EXPRESSING YOUR DELIGHT

Delight is much more than fancy. True delight must be expressed. To say "As for the saints who are in the earth, They are the majestic ones in whom is all my delight" without feeling it and showing it is hypocrisy. Here are two of many possible suggestions for expressing your delight in the saints of God. The first suggestion relates to raising the temperature of your delight in the church and her work. The second has to do with outward change.

Grow to see the bride of Christ and her work more as Jesus does. Do you see the beauty in the bride and what she does that the world cannot see? Can you see more clearly than before what Christ loves in His bride and her labors? What He loves is the increasing clarity of His own reflection in the church and her ministry. Nothing in existence or imagination can compare with the beauty of the triune God. Christ could give no greater gift or beauty than to give His bride the beauty of His holiness. He loves to see this beauty grow in the hearts and lives of His people. Can you see in the church something of what He sees? Let's take it out of the theoretical: What are three examples of the beauty of Christ's holiness that you can identify in your local church?

This coming weekend—Lord willing—I will be in Tennessee

teaching more than a hundred people how to pray through a passage of Scripture. I believe it can change their prayer lives dramatically, which means it can change everything about their lives and make them more like Jesus. The great majority of people in that area will be consumed with thoughts about a football game. Forty-eight hours afterward, however, the game will be largely forgotten and virtually meaningless to most of them. I think about this during the build-up of hype prior to each Super Bowl. At the time, it is the dominant event in our culture, and yet its impact is so short-lived. Who played in the Super Bowl just two years ago? For two weeks before that kickoff nothing else in the world seemed as important or as glorious; today it is insignificant to, if not forgotten by, those who so anticipated it. The work done for the kingdom of God, by contrast, often seems so colorless and marginal at the time, but it has a beauty and glory that the world cannot see—yet. And its impact can last forever.

It takes eyes of faith to see this, and eyes of faith can grow in their acuity. Whereas in the body one's eyes tend to weaken as a person matures, in the spiritual realm the eyes of maturing faith become sharper and more penetrating. This is akin to what Paul wrote in 2 Corinthians 4:16: "Even though our outward man is perishing, yet the inward man is being renewed day by day." Those whose spiritual vision is becoming clearer will increasingly see the splendor and value of the work of the church versus the things that are passing away. And what looks so powerful and impressive to the world begins to appear weak and pale to the maturing Christian.

The more your eyes perceive Jesus' bride and her work in the way that He does, the more you will love her and it as He does.

Demonstrate your delight in the bride of Christ in ways that will make a real difference. The work of the local church is the work of Jesus in the world. How can anyone place a low priority on involvement with the work of Christ and think he or she is becoming more like Christ?

Where does the church of Christ that you attend need help? Chances are it makes its needs known regularly. Are you listening? Can't find your niche? Then take the initiative and create a ministry. Look for the delight found in hidden and unheralded places of service. Pursue the secret glory concealed in the mundane ministries. Give your heart and time and money and zeal to the bride for whom Christ gave His life. How long should you do this? For as long as you can say of those who have the Spirit of God, "They are the majestic ones in whom is all my delight." And for as long as Christ loves His bride.

This is how you will help to build what will last. Contrary to what man builds, "whatever God does, it shall be forever" (Ecclesiastes 3:14). Regardless of how despised or irrelevant the work of the church appears in the eyes of the world, it is a work that will gleam with God-given glory forever.

Imagine a history book written in Heaven a million years after the end of the earth. How much space will it devote to the stock market, corporate mergers, presidential elections, and sports championships? Won't it be dominated instead by actions in and through local churches, deeds that passed unnoticed at the time by people the world overlooked? The names of many mighty and noble may be mere footnotes, but the names of those who loved the Lord and ministered to His saints will fill its pages. And written in gold letters on the flyleaf may be this inscription, "For God is not unjust to forget your work and labor of love which you have shown toward His name, in that you have ministered to the saints, and do minister" (Hebrews 6:10).

Psalm 149:4 tells us that "the LORD takes pleasure in His people." Do you?

ARE THE SPIRITUAL DISCIPLINES INCREASINGLY IMPORTANT TO YOU?

WE HAD A WOOD-BURNING STOVE INSTALLED AT THE WHITNEY house last year. I've written much of this book on a yellow pad, using a fountain pen, while sitting in my stoveside chair. When you use a woodstove, you learn what it means to *build* a fire.

First I crumple several sheets of newspaper into "bouquets," tightly wadded at the bottom (for slower burning) and flared at the top (for instant flame). Upon these I layer a dozen or so strips of tinder. These are dry, thin pieces of wood between the size of a physician's tongue depressor and a paint-stirring stick. After I've made sure the damper is open and the vent in front is set for maximum airflow, I strike a long, wooden match. Reaching into the stove, I touch several spots in rapid succession where the paper will light quickly. To increase the draft temporarily, I close the door within an inch of shutting it completely. The flames spread to the balled paper, which burns long enough to ignite the tinder. These pieces are burning well by the time the paper turns to ashes. Now I'm wearing fireplace gloves and ready to lay on a few sticks of kindling, which are roughly the thickness of a hammer handle, though often a little longer. When several of these are flaming happily atop the small, pulsing coals of the tinder, the stove is ready for the first of the full-size hunks of wood that will warm me all evening. The first flash of match and paper is bright and impressive, but the reason I build the fire is to enjoy the sustained heat of burning logs and slow-glowing coals.

Perhaps you are like a Christian woman I know who sometimes wonders if she is still growing spiritually, because the original God-kindled blaze of eternal life that once illuminated the darkness of her life so suddenly, seldom flames up as dramatically as when she was first converted. But what is true for the woodstove is true in this case for the Christian heart as well: just because the beginning of the combustion may briefly be more spectacular than at present doesn't mean the fire isn't growing. The initial burst of spiritual flame may be more dazzling, but the heartfire's greatest effectiveness occurs as it burns into consistency.

Nothing contributes to the growth of spiritual heat and light more than the persevering practice of the Christian spiritual disciplines. The disciplines are the bellows and the iron poker—tools in God's hands through which He stokes and blows upon the eternal fire He Himself ignites in His people.

WHAT ARE THE
SPIRITUAL DISCIPLINES?

The spiritual disciplines are the God-ordained means by which we bring ourselves before God, experience Him, and are changed into Christlikeness. The Lord is omnipresent and we often encounter Him in unexpected places and surprising ways. Nevertheless, it has pleased Him to establish specific means—the spiritual disciplines—whereby we may expect to encounter Him regularly and be transformed by Him. If the Lord might be compared to a pure, life-giving river, the spiritual disciplines would be those ways by which we come to the river to drink from, dive into, swim in, eat from, wash with, and irrigate with it.

These devotional and sanctifying practices have been categorized in many ways. One approach classifies them as personal and corporate (or congregational) disciplines, meaning some disciplines are practiced in isolation, others are practiced in community. Examples of the former are the private reading of and meditating on Scripture, individual prayer, fasting, solitude, and the keeping of a spiritual journal. Disciplines that require the presence of others include congregational worship, corporate prayer, the Lord's Supper, and fellowship. Many of the disciplines taught in the Bible can be practiced both alone *and* with the church. For instance, we can study the Bible on our own and with a group. Service for Christ's sake can be practiced individually as well as collectively. The same is true with evangelism and Christian learning.[1]

Keep in mind that the spiritual disciplines are *biblical,* that is, God-given and found in His written Word. Whatever else might be said about them, those practices originating from ourselves, derived from the culture, or discovered in other religions may not properly be considered Christian spiritual disciplines.

Remember also that the spiritual disciplines found in Christian Scripture are *sufficient.* God has revealed in the pages of the Bible every devotional and transformational practice necessary. No other ceremony, rite, ritual, religious habit, or spiritual exercise is needed for progress in Christ's likeness.

Moreover, the Spirit of God works through *each* of these disciplines *in unique ways.* What He gives through one discipline He does not duplicate in another. You cannot receive through a prayer meeting the identical blessings given through fasting, and vice versa. All the Christian spiritual disciplines are important and singularly beneficial. A discipline neglected is a blessing unclaimed.

Recognize, too, that the spiritual disciplines are *practices, not attitudes.* Do not confuse them with character qualities, Christian graces, or "the fruit of the Spirit" (Galatians 5:22-23). Prayer is a spiritual discipline; love—strictly speaking—is not. Faithful stewardship of your time and money is a discipline in a way that joy isn't. Although we must never *separate* the external practices known as the spiritual disciplines from the internal realities that are their impulse and power, we may *distinguish* them.

WHY SHOULD I PRACTICE THE SPIRITUAL DISCIPLINES?

All who consider themselves Christians are exhorted in Hebrews 12:14 to "Pursue . . . holiness, without which no one will see the Lord." Pursuing holiness is not what qualifies us to "see the Lord"; it is the Lord Himself who qualifies us for this by grace through faith in the life and death of Jesus Christ. Rather the ongoing pursuit of holiness (in other words, sanctification, godliness, Christlikeness) is characteristic of everyone who is on the way to "see the Lord" in Heaven.

Without exception, all who have been given the *Holy* Spirit will pursue *holi*ness. His holy presence and holy ministry within us cause us to love holiness, to long for it, and at times to grieve over our lack of it. The Bible doesn't set a minimum acceptable speed for the pursuit of holiness, but it says plainly that without holiness "no one will see the Lord," regardless of profession of faith, church experience, goodness of life, or Bible knowledge. If no one will go to Heaven without pursuing holiness/Christlikeness/godliness, then there's hardly a more important question than, "How do we pursue it?"

"Discipline yourself," answers 1 Timothy 4:7 (NASB), "for the purpose of godliness." And the way to "discipline yourself" is to engage in the disciplines commanded and modeled in the Bible. In short, the Christian spiritual disciplines are the means to godliness, to the "holiness, without which no one will see the Lord."

This is why the title of this chapter probes your growth in holiness by asking, "Are the spiritual disciplines increasingly important to you?" Of course, it's not necessarily a mark of growth when the disciplines take a greater percentage of your daily or weekly time than they used to (though that might be very significant). What does matter is whether their *influence* continues to expand in your life. Growing Christians have a growing appetite for those things that bring the sweetest enjoyment of God.

No doubt, though, when one of the spiritual disciplines gathers the dust of disregard, to pick it up and incorporate it into your routine certainly could signify growth in godliness. If, for instance, a person is not even practicing the crucial disciplines of Bible-intake and prayer, then growth in Christlikeness would definitely involve more actual time devoted to them, for these were the practices of Christ Himself and are the basic means by which God transforms us.

Those who have believed in Jesus Christ know Him to be so gratifying and desirable that they crave to be like Him. And when you want to be like Jesus, you aspire to do what Jesus did—to live as much as possible as Jesus lived. Well, Jesus practiced the spiritual disciplines; through them He purposely placed Himself before the Father. So it follows that increased devotion to the same disciplines that Jesus practiced will accompany those who are becoming like Jesus.

However, engaging in the Christian disciplines is much more than imitating Jesus' example. The spiritual disciplines are the biblical avenues of intentional communion with Christ by those who love Him. All love craves intimacy, especially your greatest love. And as you grow more intimate with Jesus, you will obviously gravitate toward the means of that intimacy. You will not think of the disciplines as mere duty, nor simply as Christlike patterns to follow, but rather as life and light from Heaven to your soul.

Intimacy with Jesus—because His beauty is ever fresh—promotes even deeper love, which in turn intensifies your desire for closer communion. So as you grow closer to Christ, you will necessarily grow in the depth, if not duration, of your experience with what ministers Christ to you. Because the spiritual disciplines are the channels of communion with Christ, there simply will be no sustained growth in Christ without them.

WHAT ARE THE DANGERS OF THE DISCIPLINES?

Do not understand me to say that the mere rise of the disciplines in your priorities automatically indicates a rise in your likeness to Christ. Both the Pharisees of Jesus' day and the cultists of our own time are legendary for intense devotion to spiritual disciplines. The Pharisees fasted twice each week, made long prayers, and spent years learning the contents of the Scriptures of the Old Covenant. Although they devoted huge amounts of time to some of the disciplines, they did so while hating the Son of God. They were exemplary in discipline, but the epitome of ungodliness. Members of cults are likewise known to give themselves to lengthy periods of prayer and fasting and to prodigious feats of religious dedication. But apart from the presence and sanctifying work of the Spirit of God within, such efforts only render a person even more culpable at the Judgment.

The spiritual disciplines are not by themselves the *marks* of Christlikeness as much as they are the *means* to it. Without understanding this distinction, it is possible for someone to practice the disciplines and be far from Christ. A chaplain reportedly asked a famous American general in the Second World War if the presence of the Bible on his bedside table indicated that he read it. He is said to have taken the Lord's name in vain while answering that he read his Bible every day. In much the same way, even true believers can spend hours each week in the disciplines and not grow spiritually if their motive is misplaced or if they equate bare devotional activity with godliness. The disciplines are not machines that make us more like Jesus if we will just use them. Only God's grace working *through* the disciplines can transform those who practice them with eyes of faith on Him.

Besides a wrongly motivated usage of the disciplines, another danger is imbalance. Strangely enough, some of those Christians most active in church are most in need of examining their relationship to the disciplines. Remember that we are called to engage in both corporate and personal spiritual disciplines. Many believers so enthusiastically engage in the corporate disciplines that they have little time to practice the personal ones. Or perhaps they content themselves with the thought that extraordinary involvement in the corporate disciplines excuses them from the personal disciplines or even renders them superfluous. In other words, "I'm always at church and get so much there; why do I need to practice those personal disciplines?"

Serving in the church is a virtue—a corporate discipline that is practiced less and less today because more and more people have a consumer's view of the church, not a family view. But some who serve so faithfully have no time for prayer or Scripture meditation, the two most important personal disciplines to practice. I know many people quite well who are among the most conscientious workers in their churches, but who never read the Bible outside the walls of the church and who never devote themselves exclusively to prayer. Working for Christ is right; it is healthy Christianity. But working for Christ in a way that leaves insufficient time to be alone with Him and His Word is spiritually unhealthy and wrong. As much as Jesus gave Himself to the daily service of the Father, He did not neglect the refreshment of His own soul by regular communion with the Father through the personal spiritual disciplines (see Matthew 14:23; Mark 1:35; Luke 4:42).

If in public worship a person really does worship, how can he content himself with only a weekly experience when such a glorious and satisfying God can be experienced in private worship all throughout the week? How can he say after encountering the Lord and His Word on Sunday, "That's enough. I don't need any more of that for a week"? How can that worshiper be a growing Christian? Jonathan Edwards was even more pessimistic: "If persons . . . are often highly affected when with others, and but little moved when they have none but God and Christ to converse with, it looks very darkly upon their religion."[2] Even a corpse can be made warm by the fire of another. But those who have been made alive to God also have a fire within them—the Holy Spirit who kindles the flame of their love for God every day of the week.

At the other extreme, those submerged in their own private "spirituality" need the balance of the corporate disciplines. While God-centered solitude and the other personal spiritual disciplines are essential for growth in Christlikeness, so are public worship and prayer, fellowship, service to and with other believers, the hearing of God's Word preached, and the communion of saints around the Lord's Supper, just as we find in the practice of Christ's people in the New Testament. Any who think it pleases God for them to seek Him in private while rejecting His people are greatly mistaken.

WHAT SHOULD I DO?

In one sense I've answered that question with book-length responses elsewhere (see note 1). Let me here make three suggestions that are always appropriate.

Devote yourself more to the pursuit of Christlikeness and the enjoyment of God through the spiritual disciplines than to the pursuit of efficiency and the completion of to-do lists. The increasing pace of life and the inexorable roll of "progress" in our culture foster neither the growth of the soul nor the improvement of relationships, either with God or with others (including family, fellow believers, and the lost). In our frustrating and futile efforts to keep up the demands of life maintenance, our souls have shriveled. We have more tasks, activities, and deadlines to accomplish than ever; we have more to organize, store, and maintain than ever; and the result is that we're becoming increasingly efficient at leading meaningless lives. What good is our multitasking, the accomplishment of more and more, and the acquisition of wealth, if we are not—by the means God has given us—becoming more like Jesus, the One we live for and the One who will evaluate our lives?

Resist the temptation to believe in microwave spirituality or shortcut Christlikeness. The subtitle of James Gleick's popular book *Faster* is *The acceleration of just about everything.*[3] One thing that will always be an exception to acceleration is the rate of growth in godliness. The increasing speed of our machines cannot stimulate a corresponding rate in the growth of our souls. Faster Internet connections do not make us like Jesus more quickly. Theologian R. C. Sproul emphasized, "There are no quick and easy paths to spiritual maturity. The soul that seeks a deeper level of maturity must be prepared for a long, arduous task. If we are to seek the kingdom of God, we must abandon any formulae that promise instant spiritual gratification."[4] But whatever time and effort is required, the pursuit of intimacy with and likeness to Jesus Christ is worth it all.

Stoke your spiritual life with at least one perceptible poke. When a well-wooded fire in my stove burns low, usually a good nudge or two with the iron poker restores its vitality. Having now invested part of your life to read this chapter, don't turn from it without choosing at least one sharp spiritual discipline to make at least one noticeable nudge in the fire of your soul's growth.

CHAPTER EIGHT

I AM CONVINCED THAT THE FIRST STEP TOWARDS
ATTAINING A HIGHER STANDARD OF HOLINESS IS TO
REALIZE MORE FULLY THE AMAZING SINFULNESS OF
SIN.
—J. C. RYLE

DO YOU STILL
GRIEVE OVER SIN?

IN 1725, THE YEAR BEFORE HE SETTLED IN NORTHAMPTON,
Massachusetts, to help his grandfather pastor the church there,
a young Jonathan Edwards wrote:

> I have had a vastly greater sense of my own wicked-
> ness, and the badness of my heart, than ever I had
> before my conversion. It has often appeared to me that
> if God should mark iniquity against me I should
> appear the very worst of all mankind—of all that have
> been, since the beginning of the world to this time,
> and that I should have by far the lowest place in hell.
> My wickedness, as I am in myself, has long
> appeared to me perfectly ineffable, and swallowing up
> all thought and imagination; like an infinite deluge or

mountains over my head. I know not how to express better what my sins appear to me to be than by heaping infinite upon infinite, and multiplying infinite by infinite. Very often, for these many years, these expressions are in my mind, and in my mouth, "Infinite upon infinite . . . Infinite upon infinite!" When I look into my heart, and take a view of my wickedness, it looks like an abyss infinitely deeper than hell.[1]

Is this normal, healthy Christianity? Or is this obsessive, unnecessary groveling? I believe that Edwards' words of grief over his sin not only indicate that he was growing in grace, but also that all growing Christians think and feel as Edwards did. Here's what I mean.

WHEN TO GRIEVE IS TO GROW

The closer you get to Christ, the more you will hate sin; for nothing is more unlike Christ than sin. Because Jesus hates sin, the more like Him you grow the more you will grow to hate sin. And the more you hate sin, the more you will grieve whenever you realize that you have embraced that which killed your Savior.

Perhaps the world has never seen a man closer to Christ than the apostle Paul in the final years of his life. And yet, having grown into such a universally recognized example of Christlikeness, having audibly heard the voice of the Lord Himself on several occasions (see Acts 9:1-6; 18:8-10), having been given the privilege of glimpsing the glories of Heaven itself (see 2 Corinthians 12:2-4), Paul wrote in one of his final letters, "Christ Jesus came into the world to save sinners, of whom I am chief" (1 Timothy 1:15). If, as I am sure he did, Paul believed this sincerely, then he could not say it coldly. He meant every word of it with a breast-beating grief over his sin.

I once heard seminary professor John Hannah say, "The closer one comes to Christ, in one sense the more miserable he becomes."[2] Those who have a Holy-Spirit-implanted love for holy truth, holy things, and the Holy One can't help but feel miserable when they are reminded of that which is unholy within them. Sometimes the growing Christian sinks under a sense of sin so miserable that he wishes he could tear open his chest, rip out his sin-blackened heart, and fling it as far from himself as possible.

But the fact that there is a struggle with sin, and a sense of grief because of sin, is good. Unbelievers have no such struggles or griefs. They may disappoint themselves for not living up to their own standards or to the standard of someone they respect. But they do not agonize over being unholy before God—a God who is holy and who calls them to holiness (see 1 Peter 1:15). As A. W. Pink explained, "It is not the absence of sin but the grieving over it which distinguishes the child of God from empty professors [of faith]."[3]

Are you aware of sins in your life that you weren't cognizant of years ago, even though you were committing those sins back then as well? As discouraging as the fresh exposure is, and as grievous as it may be to have ever-deeper layers of sin laid bare, there's something positive here. Increased sensitivity to your sin is a mark of growth. You've made spiritual progress beyond where you were years ago because back then you didn't even realize that those *were* sins. The closer you come to the light of Christ, the more sins His holy light will expose in you. In the words of nineteenth century Bible scholar Thomas D. Bernard, "Our sense of sin is in proportion to our nearness to God."[4]

Edwards was right: "The more a true saint loves God . . . the more he mourns for sin."[5]

SHOULD I CONTINUALLY GRIEVE OVER SIN?

A longtime friend of my wife and I sent an e-mail recently. In it she wondered:

Is it good to always be so aware of my sin rather than focusing solely on the love and grace of God? After all, isn't that counterproductive now that we have been forgiven? And if someone has a tendency to be overly introspective or easily discouraged, can't the frequent thought of your sinfulness push you too far toward guilt and gloom?

Excessive introspection is itself a sinful possibility. But the spirit of the age certainly doesn't incline us to go to extremes in brooding over our sin. Even at church, religious entertainment characterizes more "worship" services than conviction of sin. Sermons are much more likely to be described as upbeat than heart-searching. Guffaws are far more common in church than tears, whether tears of joy *or* of repentance.

True, the correct proportion must be assigned to both the occasions of sin in a Christian's life and the incomparable freedom of forgiveness and grace he has through Christ. It is also true that many ministers and churches overemphasize the wrath of God and the sinfulness of people, including God-forgiven people. Nevertheless, amid all the error or overemphasis on sin a person may have experienced, and despite all the joy in the Lord that should characterize a Christian, the truth remains that the more a believer in Christ experiences growth, the more he grieves over sin. As Edwards put it in *Religious Affections:* "One great difference between saints and hypocrites is this, that the joy and comfort of the former is attended with godly sorrow and mourning for sin."[6]

Jesus Himself describes true Christians not only as those who *have* mourned over their sin, but also as those who are *still* mourning: "Blessed are those who mourn [present tense], for they shall be comforted" (Matthew 5:4). This is not to say that Christians should be mourning their sin every moment, but it does mean that they should grieve over it all their lives. We do not read of the apostle Paul endlessly lamenting his sin. Often we find him greatly rejoicing, not grieving, such as when we read of him singing praise to God at midnight with Silas in the Philippian jail (see Acts 16:25). On the other hand, he wouldn't think of himself near the end of his life as the "chief" sinner on the planet unless there had been much private grief over the sins that prompted such a claim.

There is a widely mistaken notion that repentance and faith in Christ are once-only events. Thereafter, when hearing of these matters, we tend to think, "I've done that." But Christians are *lifelong* repenters and *lifelong* believers. The initial experiences of turning from sin and trusting in Christ should characterize every Christian every day to some extent. Not that the new birth should occur daily for the child of God, for that happens only once. Rather the first experiences of those newly born again— repentance and faith—are the daily stuff of Christian living.

Jeremiah Burroughs, one of the most beloved of the seventeenth-century English Puritan preachers, elaborates in his book on sin, *The Evil of Evils*:

> There's a great mistake in the world in the matter of trouble for sin. They think repentance or mourning for sin is but one act, that if once they have been troubled for sin they need never be troubled anymore. It is a dangerous mistake, for we need to know that true sorrow for sin, true repentance, is a continual act that must abide all our lives. And it is not only at that time when we are afraid that God will not pardon our sins, when we are afraid that we shall be damned for our sins, but when we come to hope that God will, yes, when we come to know that God has pardoned our sins.[7]

Because, therefore, a Christian is always looking afresh to Christ and often turning from sin, it follows that he would often grieve over the presence of this sin. Would true repentance, simply by virtue of its frequency, become heartless and mechanical?

God forbid! Lifelong repentance of sin implies some measure of lifelong grief for sin.

THE RIGHT AND WRONG WAY TO GRIEVE OVER SIN

In 2 Corinthians 7:8-11 the Bible juxtaposes two kinds of sorrow for sin: one that is expressed "in a godly manner" and then a "sorrow of the world." The passage contrasts the "godly sorrow" as the kind that by God's grace leads to salvation with the worldly sorrow that does not result in biblical repentance. Even unbelievers can grieve over sin, but without it being "in a godly manner," that is, without it leading to the proper end—repentance and its fruits. Still, as those who have experienced the "godly sorrow" that leads to eternal life, believers can either grieve over sin as Christians ought, or improperly as worldlings do.

Godly sorrow is much more than admitting your imperfections. I've never met anyone who considered himself perfect, but relatively few are often brokenhearted because they know themselves to be nonstop offenders against the Law of God. Many professing Christians show no more sorrow for sin on their occasional or perfunctory confessions to God than a boy forced to say "I'm sorry" to his sister. As a child of God, should we feel no more deeply about our sin than this? Godly sorrow for sin does involve *sorrow*.

Godly sorrow also results in repentance, that is, a change of mind about the sin that produces a change of behavior. The apostle Paul had written to the Christians in Corinth regarding sin and he later rejoiced in this result: "Now I rejoice, not that you were made sorry [only], but that your sorrow led to repentance" (2 Corinthians 7:9). Contrast their grief for sin with the kind manifested by Esau, the brother of the Old Testament patriarch Isaac: "He could bring about no change of mind though he sought the blessing with tears" (Hebrews 12:17, NIV). Like Esau, we may weep with regret over our sins and yet have no change of mind and life, no real repentance. Godly sorrow involves true sorrow, but true sorrow without true repentance is not godly sorrow. In addition, sorrow for sin that is "in a godly manner" is genuinely humble. Edwards reflected on how some who use the most self-effacing language to describe their sinfulness may also be the most proud:

"I am a poor vile creature," they may say, "I am not worthy of the least mercy, or that God should look upon me! Oh, I have a dreadful wicked heart! My heart is worse than the devil! Oh, this cursed heart of mine, etc." Such expressions are very often used, not with a heart that is broken. . . . There are many that are full of expressions of their own vileness, who yet expect to be looked upon as eminent and bright saints by others, as their due.[8]

Godly sorrow in the growing Christian makes him a thousand times more aware of his pride than his humility. It sometimes causes him to wonder how God's saving grace and such pride could dwell in the same heart. His grief is such that he feels himself to be "less than the least of all the saints" (Ephesians 3:8), not a great one at all.

In the worldly sort of grief for sin, the focus is on self. Like Esau, it may betray self-pity over what has been lost as a consequence of sin (see Genesis 25:27-34; 27:36-38). It may reveal self-disappointment over the failure to keep one's own standards or those of one's family or church. Worldly sorrow may even include a self-centered fear of God's wrath or of hell. While it's right to fear these, they may be feared only out of concern for self and without any thought of God, without any grief over having offended God.

All worldly grief over sin is itself sin because its main interest is selfward. Against this, Burroughs wrote:

The chief of all is the humiliation of the soul for sin as
it is against God. Then is the heart humbled rightly for
sin when it apprehends how, by sin, the soul has been
against the infinite, glorious First-Being of all things.
All other humiliations in the world are not sufficient
without this. For it is not deep enough. There can be no
humiliation deep enough unless the soul is humbled
for sin because it has sinned against God.[9]

King David was a great sinner, but God called him "a man
after My own heart" (Acts 13:22) because he was also a great
repenter. Notice the God-centeredness of his grief: "Against You,
You only, have I sinned, and done this evil in Your sight—that
You may be found just when You speak, and blameless when
You judge" (Psalm 51:4). The entire Psalm is addressed to God
and overflows with thirty-one specific references to Him in just
nineteen verses. As David's example shows, godly sorrow is *Godward* sorrow. And when our focus is on God and not self, we can
hope for grace and pray expectantly with David, "Restore to me
the joy of Your salvation, and uphold me by Your generous
Spirit" (Psalm 51:12).

There is another measure of gentle sweetness in a Christian's
godly grief over sin. Godly sorrow is the misery of a lover pining for what will be. We grieve over our sin partly because we
long so for a holiness that is coming, but not yet. Paul writes in
Romans 8:23, "We also who have the firstfruits of the Spirit,
even we ourselves groan within ourselves, eagerly waiting for the
adoption, the redemption of our body." The presence of the
Holy Spirit in an unholy creature causes longings for what we
are promised but do not have—thoroughly holy hearts and
holy minds living in holy bodies. Because of His residence, we
groan over every painful reminder that holiness is not yet, that
we are still awaiting what God has destined us to become—the
likeness of His sinless Son (see Romans 8:29-30).

WHAT SHOULD I DO IF I
DO NOT GRIEVE OVER SIN?

John Owen ventured, "I do not understand how a man can be a true believer in whom sin is not the greatest burden, sorrow, and trouble."[10] If you are not sure your experience resonates with Owen's statement, consider the following recommendations:

Make sure you understand the gospel of the New Testament. I'm always amazed at how many churchgoing people are unclear on the gospel. Write it out, as if you were putting it in a letter or e-mail. Think paragraph or page length, not a sentence or two. In this instance, give special attention to two parts of the gospel: that which made the death of Jesus necessary, and the relationship of repentance to faith.

Ask God to show you the reality of your sin. Ask Him to show you specifics of how you sin, when you sin, where you sin, why you sin, and against whom you sin.

Pray slowly through Psalm 51, making it your own heartfelt prayer. Remember that these words are more than just David's words. God Himself inspired them (see 2 Timothy 3:16), and He preserved them as an example of grief over sin. Pray through these words until they become a reflection of your own heart.

Meditate on the fact that it was your sin that nailed the holy, sinless One from Heaven to the cross. Are you never sorrowful for causing the death of Jesus? Think of what your sin cost the most pure, loving, and gracious One who ever lived. Consider how others are now in hell for the same sins you've committed. Remember that it is the eternal and perfect law of God Himself that you have so willingly and repeatedly broken and disregarded. Realize that your every sin is a double sin because every sin is also a failure to keep the greatest of all commandments—to love God with all your heart, soul, mind, and strength (see Mark 12:28-30). "Behold the Man" (John 19:5) your sins have pierced. Then remember that the life and death of Jesus saves from sin all who repent and believe. Be driven closer to Christ by your sin. May your sin only serve to cause you to prize Christ even more.

Preach the gospel to yourself every day. I've borrowed this phrase from Jerry Bridges, who wrote:

> To preach the gospel to yourself, then, means that you continually face up to your own sinfulness and then flee to Jesus through faith in His shed blood and righteous life. It means that you appropriate, again by faith, the fact that Jesus fully satisfied the law of God, that he is your propitiation, and that God's holy wrath is no longer directed toward you. . . . You can be sure of one thing, though: When you set yourself to seriously pursue holiness, you will begin to realize what an awful sinner you are. And if you are not firmly rooted in the gospel and have not learned to preach it to yourself every day, you will soon become discouraged and will slack off in your pursuit of holiness.[11]

From this perspective of grieving for sin, there are two ways to evaluate your life—proximity to the ideal or progress toward it. You can look at what you ought to be—Christlike—and be discouraged because you are so far from it. Too much measuring yourself by the perfection of Jesus will dishearten you. Too little can breed spiritual pride. But you can also look at how far by God's grace you've come, and be hopeful. In the life of the growing Christian, there are times for both.

THE UNFORGIVING SPIRIT . . . IS THE NUMBER ONE
KILLER OF SPIRITUAL LIFE.

ARE YOU A QUICKER FORGIVER?

I WAS TWENTY-SEVEN WHEN I BECAME THE PASTOR OF A SMALL RURAL church in a southern state. I was the seventeenth pastor of that church in twenty-one years. Today that statistic tells me far more than it did when I was twenty-seven.

Although I'd grown up in a small-town church in the same state, I had no idea in those days how horribly some churches treat pastors, no matter how hard-working or loving the ministers may be. I assumed that if I loved the people, preached the Word of God to them, and gave myself to serve them, they all would respond well and be grateful. That was the most naïve mistake of my life.

A woman I'll call Patsy increasingly opposed me. Disagreement deteriorated into criticism. The criticisms became more caustic until they spewed forth in confrontive, brazen challenges. "If you had the faith you preach about," she once taunted, "you'd leave [with no place to go or to live] and trust God to provide for you." When, after twelve months, I spent my first week away from the church, she managed to arrange a meeting of some of the deacons for the purpose of getting me fired. Later she admitted "forgetting" to call those deacons who were known to be my strong supporters.

Despite her desire to see me go, when she heard second-hand that while on vacation I had interviewed with another church, she called that church and misrepresented herself in an effort to find out what I'd been doing. After I returned she asked if I'd be willing to come to a Saturday night meeting (that she had already secretly organized) "to discuss some problems in the church." I was the pastor; how could I not go?

Upon arrival I learned that I was there as the accused to stand trial and Patsy was the self-appointed prosecutor. Although most of her efforts that night were frustrated, she had done her best to humiliate me before the church and to undermine my pastoral leadership.

After fifteen months of stomach churning, the Lord opened a new door of ministry as pastor of a church where He "turned for me my mourning into dancing" (Psalm 30:11). I was there for almost fifteen years. But the stress of our pressure-cooker pastorate took its toll. Between us, Caffy and I experienced five hospitalizations, three surgeries, and the inability to have children for sixteen years.

I knew I had to be willing to forgive Patsy, but I found it hard because she had treated us in such ungodly ways. In the last month of our time there, Caffy was diagnosed with a life-threatening, stress-induced thyroid difficulty that soon required the removal of the gland. When the physician she first consulted—an unconverted man—examined her, he asked, "What are those people out there doing to you two?"

Patsy was merciless, relentless, and rapacious. Why should I forgive her? Every day for months on end, if I didn't see her in person, I saw her face in my mind. Mentally I replayed each of her attacks, only now I said the things I wished I'd said then.

I might be in my car, driving; I might be trying to sleep, or even praying, and find myself gnashing my teeth at her, even bursting out in angry shouts at the Patsy in my imagination. Often I would awaken from my imaginary conversation glaring at nothing, fists clenched, stomach acid boiling, breath coming rapidly.

I can't remember ever emerging from one of these frequent episodes without an awareness that God's will was for me to forgive Patsy. Especially when her specter would invade my prayer time I would recall Jesus' words, "And whenever you stand praying, if you have anything against anyone, forgive him, that your Father in heaven may also forgive you your trespasses. But if you do not forgive, neither will your Father in heaven forgive your trespasses" (Mark 11:25-26).

I knew it was useless to pray unless I forgave Patsy. It was one thing for her to accuse me of failures as a pastor; it was another for my own conscience to accuse me before God because of her.

But at last I found the grace to let go of my bitterness. I realized that I could either continue to stoke my smoldering grudge against her and allow her to control me in absentia, or I could move toward forgiveness just as I had been forgiven by Jesus.

REAL CHRISTIANS WANT TO FORGIVE

Although my heart was a volcano of anger, by God's grace I was also inclined to forgive Patsy. I knew forgiveness to be the will of God, as well as the path back to freedom and joy. When God makes of us "a new creation" (2 Corinthians 5:17), He gives us a disposition to love and obey His will (as in Psalm 40:8). And this heart desire to do God's will—such as to forgive—beats within us even during the times when we sinfully resist it.

Three times in the Gospels Jesus directly connects our forgiveness of others with God's forgiveness of us—Mark 11:25-26 (quoted previously), Matthew 6:14-15, and also Luke 6:37, where He says, "Forgive, and you will be forgiven." He did not mean that we earn God's forgiveness for the sins we commit against Him by granting forgiveness to others for their sins against us. This would make our salvation conditional upon doing something to earn it—in this case dispensing forgiveness to others. Rather, these texts show that *a forgiving spirit characterizes those who have been forgiven.* Repenters toward God are forgivers toward others. Those who find themselves unable to forgive reveal that they've never experienced the transforming forgiveness of God. But those who are willing to forgive as God forgives may be hopeful that they have received the grace of God. And this grace causes them to truly *want* to forgive, even when the flesh rages against that impulse.

In Matthew 18:21-35, Jesus told a parable about a king and one of his servants. The servant owed an unpayable debt, but the king showed great mercy and forgave the entire amount. When the king heard that the servant had choked a fellow servant to wring from him a tiny unpaid debt, he was enraged: "You wicked servant! I forgave you all that debt because you begged me. Should you not also have had compassion on your fellow servant, just as I had pity on you?" (verses 32-33). He then condemned the servant to prison where he would spend his remaining years in a futile attempt to work off the impossible debt.

Then Jesus made His point: "So My heavenly Father also will do to you if each of you, from his heart, does not forgive his brother his trespasses" (verse 35). Unlike the servant in the story, the true servant of God will be a forgiver. Knowing that God has forgiven him a debt of sin he could never remove, he is willing to forgive others. And the grace of God causes him to want to forgive another's comparatively insignificant sins against him, not just with words but "from his heart."

The testimony of Martyn Lloyd-Jones should be the heart-cry of every Christian: "I say to the glory of God and in utter humility that whenever I see myself before God and realize even something of what my blessed Lord has done for me, I am ready to forgive anybody anything."[1]

READY TO FORGIVE VERSUS EXTENDING FORGIVENESS

Notice Lloyd-Jones' phrase, "I am *ready* to forgive anybody anything" (emphasis added). Many do not understand the difference between being ready to forgive and actually extending forgiveness.

Often after a shooting at a school or some other horrendous, large-scale massacre, well-meaning spokespeople in the community will appeal for people to forgive the murderer(s). But biblical forgiveness is never given or required where there is no repentance. Although Jesus prayed immediately after they nailed Him to a cross, "Father, forgive them, for they do not know what they do" (Luke 23:34), this wasn't an unconditional forgiveness. Otherwise these people would be forgiven of their sins without repenting and believing in the gospel—a heretical notion. "On the cross, Jesus did not forgive," Jay Adams points out, "He prayed." Referring to the martyr Stephen's prayer for the forgiveness of his persecutors in Acts 7:60, Adams continues,

> The same is true of Stephen. If forgiveness is unconditional, Jesus, Stephen, and others would have *forgiven* their murderers rather than use what, if true, would be a roundabout way to do so. At other times Jesus had no hesitancy in saying, "Your sins be forgiven you."
>
> Jesus' prayer was answered in the response to the preaching of Peter and the apostles on the day of Pentecost, and on those other occasions when thousands of Jews repented and believed the Gospel (Acts 2:37-38; 3:17-19; 4:4). They were not forgiven the

sin of crucifying the Savior apart from believing that
He was dying for their sins, but precisely by doing so
in response to the faithful preaching of the Gospel in
Jerusalem.[2]

What Christians should always do, as Jesus exemplified in
His prayer, is be *ready* to forgive. And then, when forgiveness is
sought, forgiveness can be extended.

Yes, we ought to release our sinful bitterness and hatred
whether the offender ever seeks forgiveness. Some equate this
decision with forgiveness itself. In reality though, this is only
getting ready, being willing to forgive. Then if the offender
repents, we are prepared to complete the process by saying, "I forgive you." The one who announces forgiveness where it hasn't
been sought not only discounts the importance of repentance, he
also misunderstands the requirement of Scripture. But the one
who is not willing to forgive is contradicting the Scripture, and
for the moment at least, is putting the reality of his salvation to
the test.

Leon Morris, a New Testament scholar from Australia,
noted, "We can always think of some 'good' reason why in any
particular case we need not forgive. But that is always an error."[3]
Growing Christians will recognize that error and become
quicker to say to themselves, "I'm ready to forgive."

FORGIVE AND FORGET?

The Bible doesn't contain the expression "forgive and forget."
Not only that, the Bible never commands us to forget an offense
once we have forgiven it, though sometimes forgetfulness does
result from forgiveness.

The promise of God for all who know Him through Christ
is "I will forgive their iniquity, and their sin I will remember no
more" (Jeremiah 31:34). Because God is omniscient, knowing

infallibly all the past, present, and future, He doesn't actually forget our sins. What His forgiveness means is that He will not remember them *against* us anymore. He will never bring them up again. That's the way we are to forgive others. To say "I forgive you" is not a commitment never to recall the offense, but forgiveness *is* a promise never to *use* the sin against the offender again. While we may not totally forget the offense, we are to treat the forgiven person as though we *had* forgotten it. (There may be occasions where trust needs to be rebuilt after a wrongdoing is forgiven, but forgiveness means that the offense itself will never again be the basis of a breach in the relationship.)

When I first overcame my unwillingness to forgive Patsy, it was like pulling an enemy's flaming arrow out of my chest. The removal initially seemed worse than the torment of living with the bitterness. Immediately after the extraction, however, my soul began to breathe more easily and a cleansing process began.

Not all the poison of bitterness was removed from my system immediately. Although I had passed the greatest crisis of forgiveness, her face soon reappeared in my mind and with it the mental videotapes of many of our confrontations. Here I began to learn for the first time that the readiness to forgive might not always be won in a single decisive battle. I truly wanted to forgive Patsy, but when in my mind I relived her attacks, the wounds were reopened.

Jesus teaches us, "Take heed to yourselves. If your brother sins against you, rebuke him; and if he repents, forgive him. And if he sins against you seven times in a day, and seven times in a day returns to you, saying, 'I repent,' you shall forgive him" (Luke 17:3-4). We're to take this literally; that is, we should be willing to forgive the repentant believer no matter how often he sincerely repents. But I think it would be rather unusual for a person to come in sincere humility seven times to repent for a sin willfully committed on seven different occasions in one day. And yet, when I have been offended it is not unusual at all for the *memory* of that one offense to return to my mind seven times in a single day. Just as in the situation Jesus described, I might find myself faced with the necessity to become willing to forgive at least seven times that day.

That's the way it was with my frequent recollections of Patsy's hurtful attacks. With each remembrance I had to return to the cross of Jesus and renew my willingness to forgive her. And while the fresh tearing of the wound made the process painful, the second time wasn't quite as difficult as the first, for there had been some progress in healing. The third time was less difficult than the second, and each succeeding time I had to return to this crisis of forgiveness was easier than the previous one. It wasn't long until I could think of Patsy without bitterness at all. And though she never sought my forgiveness, by God's grace I reached the place where I was ready to give it.

I believe it is because I became willing to forgive Patsy that I have virtually forgotten the things she said and did. However, sometimes we may believe we have fulfilled God's expectation of forgiveness simply because we no longer think of the offenses. In other words, life goes on, we become occupied with other things, and eventually we forget without forgiving. But even worldlings can do that. Does the return of a seldom-remembered face or event cause your stomach to churn and your jaw muscles to tighten? *Be careful that you do not think you have forgiven just because you have forgotten.*

PROBING THE HEART

"Everyone thinks forgiveness is a lovely idea," C. S. Lewis observed, "until he has something to forgive."[4] If you don't have something to forgive at present, you soon will. Here are three personal inquiries intended to encourage you to do what every Christian, by grace, wants to do "from his heart."

Are you ready to forgive? Perhaps this is better asked in

reverse: Is there anyone you are *not* ready to forgive? Is there anyone at church, at work, in your neighborhood, or in your family whose face or voice causes more of the acid of bitterness to flow out of your heart than the willingness to forgive? If so, resolving that matter is the only way forward. As King David testified in Psalm 86:5, the Lord is "ready to forgive." To grow more like Him means that we must be likewise, and in every situation.

Do you need to initiate the process of forgiveness with anyone? If you know you are the offender, the next step is clear. Repent—don't merely apologize, repent—for your offense and ask forgiveness. During my final two weeks as Patsy's pastor, I became convicted of my sin of gossiping about her sins. I tried to reason my way around asking her forgiveness by telling myself that her sins were 95 percent of the problem between us, and that my gossip was only 5 percent of the sin in this matter. But I knew that regardless of what she did, I was responsible before God for my 5 percent and had to repent. It wasn't easy to go to Patsy and ask her forgiveness. I knew that my confession likely would result only in Patsy feeling more justified in her opposition to me and in her having more ammunition to use against me. Still, I wanted to do what I believed was right in God's sight and leave the consequences to Him.

You may also need to initiate the process of forgiveness with someone who has offended you. Jesus said, "If your brother sins against you, rebuke him; and if he repents, forgive him" (Luke 17:3). As obvious as the sin is to you, it is possible that the offender isn't even aware that you've been offended. In any case, if you find yourself unable to overlook the offense and to practice 1 Peter 4:8, that is, "love will cover a multitude of sins," then your responsibility is to bring the offense to the person's attention and work toward reconciliation.

Do you love forgiveness? Many professing Christians are too easily offended. Some almost seem to take pride in their ability to hold a grudge or in their refusal to humble themselves or in their resistance to seeking or extending forgiveness. True Christians love forgiveness. Because of God's forgiveness of them, they think it beautiful and Godlike to give or get forgiveness. That's why the ready willingness to forgive is such a clear mark of growth in godliness. As the godly and persecuted fifth-century preacher John Chrysostom concluded, "Nothing causes us to so nearly resemble God as the forgiveness of injuries."[5]

CHAPTER TEN

YOU MAY JUDGE OF A MAN BY WHAT HE GROANS AFTER.

—C. H. SPURGEON

DO YOU YEARN FOR HEAVEN AND TO BE WITH JESUS?

As A YOUNG PASTOR, I WAS SOMETIMES FRUSTRATED BY THE EMPHASIS that elderly church members placed on Heaven. *What about now?* I wondered. *Don't you have any goals for your spiritual life, your church, or the kingdom of God at large before you die?* Now that I am nearing twice the age when I mentally muttered those semi-disparaging thoughts and am much closer to the age of the folks to whom I directed them, I am tempted to believe those thoughts were merely the musings of a zealous, but immature minister.

Those who have been on a long pilgrimage increasingly desire to reach their destination, especially one as glorious and excellent as Heaven. Those who have spent decades loving and living for Jesus naturally long to see Him. While it's obvious that such anticipation should characterize those older believers living right on the borders of Heaven, these yearnings surge in the hearts of all growing Christians.

GROWING CHRISTIANS ARE
GROANING CHRISTIANS

In Romans 8:22-23, the apostle Paul calls attention to the groans of the entire creation, and especially the groans of that human part of creation indwelled by the Spirit of God, as they await the removal of the corruption they have endured since sin's entrance into the world. He wrote, "For we know that the whole creation groans and labors with birth pangs together until now. Not only that, but we also who have the firstfruits of the Spirit, even we ourselves groan within ourselves, eagerly waiting for the adoption, the redemption of our body."

Notice that the human groaners here are not exceptionally committed Christians, but simply "we also who have the first-fruits of the Spirit." In other words, every Christian, every person in whom the Holy Spirit has begun an eternal work, experiences these groans "for the adoption, the redemption of [the] body." These longings for the coming great change in body and place are simply part of a normal, healthy, growing Christian life.

Paul reiterated this fact in 2 Corinthians 5:2 when he declared, "For in this [referring to our earthly bodies] we groan, earnestly desiring to be clothed with our habitation which is from heaven." Of course, the groans of the Christian are not simply for the clothing of a new, glorified body, but for all that such a transformation represents. Six verses later, Paul again uses a kind of theological shorthand when he looks forward to when we will "be present with the Lord" (verse 8). In each of these references, the apostle specifies only one aspect of the Christian's hope, but each is representative of the believer's entire experience in eternity. So when the Christian groans for the redemption of the body, he is also groaning to be in the presence of the Lord, who will redeem (that is, glorify) his body—to live in Heaven forever and to enjoy eternal fellowship with God's people.

"Okay," interjects someone, "but what is it like in daily life when a Christian yearns to be in Heaven and with Jesus?" An excerpt from the diary of David Brainerd (1718–1747) provides a good example. Brainerd was a missionary to Indians in eighteenth-century New England. He died of tuberculosis in the home of Jonathan Edwards at age twenty-nine. Edwards published *The Life and Diary of David Brainerd*, which remains a classic of Christian devotion. An entry from 1742 is typical:

> Saturday, June 12. Spent much time in prayer this morning, and enjoyed much sweetness. Felt insatiable longings after God much of the day. I wondered how poor souls do to live that have no God. The world with all its enjoyments quite vanished. I see myself very helpless, but I have a blessed God to go to. I longed exceedingly to be dissolved and to be with Christ, to behold His glory. Oh, my weak, weary soul longs to arrive at my Father's house![1]

Notice the "sweetness" and the joy that permeate Brainerd's longings. Despite the agony of separation from something much desired and the dissatisfaction with the present whenever we yearn for something yet future, the Holy Spirit intersperses both sweetness and happiness into our groans. This is what C. S. Lewis portrayed in his retelling of the myth of Cupid and Psyche in *Till We Have Faces*. Think of a Christian's longing to be in Heaven and with Jesus, as Psyche explains to her friend Orual,

> It was when I was happiest that I longed most. It was on happy days when we were up there on the hills, the three of us, with the wind and the sunshine. . . . Do you remember? The color and the smell, and looking across at the Grey Mountain in the distance? And because it was so beautiful, it set me longing, always longing. Somewhere else there must be more of it. Everything seemed to be saying, Psyche come! But I couldn't (not yet) come and I didn't know where

I was to come to. It almost hurt me. I felt like a bird in a cage when the other birds of its kind are flying home. . . . The sweetest thing in all my life has been the longing—to reach the Mountain, to find the place where all the beauty came from.[2]

Does Psyche give voice to your soul? Do you find more and more that the life you long for in Heaven seems more natural to you than the one you are living on earth? Does it seem that your deepest longings were made to be fulfilled in another world? These are the groans of a growing Christian, one who knows that God made us for glorious communion with Him and that we are never at home, never fulfilled, until we are there.

GROWING CHRISTIANS
GROAN FOR HOLINESS

As I mentioned, age and experience have tempered my evaluation of the often heavenward mindset of some of those older folks I pastored. But I remain reluctant to regard all longings for Heaven as rightly motivated. The older I get and the more easily my body fatigues, the more sympathetic I am to the desire for rest—eternal rest. But even Buddhists, Muslims, and atheists want that. There's nothing uniquely Christian about longing for an end to a wearying existence and the beginning of a new and more restful one.

In a similar way, pining for lasting relief from the cares of the world is also universal and not exclusively Christian. Every person on earth dreams of a time when he can lay his burdens down. Should we then base our confidence that we are growing in grace on the fact we want only what everyone else in the world, even self-confessed God-haters, wants?

Like the desires for rest and relief, yearning for reunion with deceased loved ones is as common among *non*Christians as

Christians. Just because someone looks forward with increased hope to seeing a child or parent or spouse in Heaven does not mean he or she is growing as a Christian. Realistically, it's no mark of faith at all, but of nothing more than natural affection. Even the eagerness to be with Jesus is not necessarily a confirmation of knowing Christ, much less of growth in His likeness. Some people want to see Jesus in the same way they would like to see the Virgin Mary or King David. Natural curiosity, or simply the desire to see someone so well known, may be the only motivation.

So the question is not merely, "Do you yearn for Heaven and to be with Jesus?" but also "For which Heaven and Jesus do you yearn?" Growing Christians increasingly long for a *holy* Heaven, not just a restful one. They look forward to *holy* relationships, not just nostalgic ones. They sigh to see a *holy* Jesus. They feel less and less at home in a sinful world because they are growing more and more homesick for a holy place, a holy people, and a God who is "holy, holy, holy" (Revelation 4:8). They ache to share in this holiness more than in Heaven's rest, relief, or reunions. Jonathan Edwards put it this way: "But neither a . . . longing to be in Heaven, nor longing to die, are in any measure so distinguishing marks of true saints, as longing after a more holy heart."[3]

In describing his own spiritual cravings, Edwards said in another place: "The Heaven I desired was a Heaven of holiness; to be with God, and to spend my eternity in divine love, and holy communion with Christ. My mind was very much taken up with contemplations of Heaven, and the enjoyments there; and living there in perfect holiness, humility and love."[4]

His younger friend David Brainerd shared Edwards' heartbeat with him and with all growing Christians. On October 26, 1744, he wrote:

> My soul was exceedingly grieved for sin, and prized, and longed after holiness; it wounded my heart

deeply, yet sweetly, to think how I had abused a kind God. I longed to be perfectly holy, that I might not grieve a gracious God; who will continue to love, not withstanding his love is abused.[5]

And a late twentieth-century biographer of Brainerd adds,

His often expressed desire to die was not merely a wish to escape the tribulations and trials of this life, although we cannot eliminate that motive altogether. For him the final state in Heaven was the supreme goal for living because it afforded final relief from the weight of sin which hung upon him.[6]

All this is consistent with Paul's description of a Christian in Romans 8:23, "Not only that, but we also who have the first-fruits of the Spirit, even we ourselves groan within ourselves, eagerly waiting for the adoption, the redemption of our body." To at last live in a body redeemed from sin, to exult in the breathtaking presence of Jesus Himself with a body, mind, and heart soaring free from any vestige of sin is the burning hope that obsesses the growing Christian's thoughts of eternity.

If there is anyone who would look forward to the "redemption of the body" more in a physical sense than a spiritual one it would be a Christian in circumstances like quadriplegic Joni Eareckson Tada. And yet, like all growing Christians, her greatest groans for the next life are more for holiness than health. I heard her attest:

People say, "You must be looking forward to Heaven," thinking I am looking forward to getting my new body. And after more than twenty-five years in a wheelchair, it's true that I am. But more than I am looking forward to my new body [she said with her voice choking with emotion] I am looking forward to a heart without sin.[7]

Elsewhere she added, "Most people will continue to think that getting a new body is my focus. But I can't wait to be clothed in righteousness, with not a trace of sin. . . . For me, that will be the best part of heaven."[8]

To be pure in heart and to see the Lord are the Christian's highest hopes and deepest groans, as Martyn Lloyd-Jones summarized:

> What are you looking for and hoping for in Heaven? Let me ask you a question that perhaps should come before that. Do you ever look forward to being in Heaven? . . . The person who looks forward to death simply wants to get out of life because of his troubles. That is not Christian; that is pagan. The Christian has a positive desire for Heaven, and therefore I ask: Do you look forward to being in Heaven? But, more than this, what do we look forward to when we get to Heaven? What is it we are desiring? Is it the rest of Heaven? Is it to be free from troubles and tribulations? Is it the peace of Heaven? Is it the joy of Heaven? All those things are to be found there, thank God; but that is not the thing to look forward to in Heaven. It is the face of God. "Blessed are the pure in heart: for they shall see God". . . to stand in the very presence of God—"To gaze and gaze on thee." Do we long for that? Is that Heaven to us? Is that the thing we want above everything else?[9]

GROWING CHRISTIANS GROAN FOR HOLINESS IN HEAVEN MORE THAN ANYTHING

Spiritually flourishing Christians answer Lloyd-Jones' final question in the affirmative: "Yes, we do long for the *holiness* of Heaven and the face of God above everything else."

In 2 Corinthians 5:2, Paul described the heavenly holiness we groan for as something we're also "earnestly desiring." Years before he penned these words he was given a glimpse of what awaits us in our holy home above (see 2 Corinthians 12:1-4). After that indescribable experience he could say things like, "But if I live on in the flesh, this will mean fruit from my labor; yet what I shall choose I cannot tell. For I am hard pressed between the two, having a desire to depart and be with Christ, which is far better" (Philippians 1:22-23). Despite all the unparalleled blessings Paul experienced as an apostle—miracles frequently coursing through his hands, dramatic conversions when he preached, angelic appearances, and so on, he knew firsthand that "to depart and be with Christ" is "far better." Not just better, "far better."

Consider again the intensity of the words "we groan, earnestly desiring," "to depart and be with Christ, which is far better." Paul wrote like a man who had not only tasted and seen that the Lord is good (Psalm 34:8), but like one who has found the holiness of the Lord eternally and irresistibly addictive. He couldn't get enough, and he groaned, "earnestly desiring" the one thing that could satisfy—the rapturous, full-faced enjoyment of God Himself.

It is incomparable, exclaimed Edwards:

> The enjoyment of God is the only happiness with which our souls can be satisfied. To go to Heaven, fully to enjoy God, is infinitely better than the most pleasant accommodations here. Fathers and mothers, husbands, wives, or children, or the company of earthly friends, are but shadows; but God is the substance. These are but scattered beams, but God is the sun. These are but streams, but God is the ocean.[10]

Brainerd also thirsted for the holy ocean of God more than he wanted anything else:

Tuesday, June 15 [1742]. Had the most ardent longings after God that ever I felt in my life. At noon in
my secret retirement I could do nothing but tell my
Lord, in a sweet calm, that He knew I longed for
nothing but Himself, nothing but holiness; that He
had given me these desires and He only could give me
the thing desired.[11]

Jesus said, "For where your treasure is, there your heart will
be also" (Matthew 6:21). When your treasure is in Heaven, like
Paul, Jonathan Edwards, David Brainerd, and all other growing
Christians, your heart will ache for Heaven more than for anything else. That's not to deny the many legitimate longings we
have for earthly things. The desires to get married, have children,
experience job satisfaction, and the like, may also be strong,
long-lasting, and God-ignited. But even if someone wanted one
or more of these as much as Joni Eareckson Tada yearns to walk,
maturing Christians would say with Joni that year in and year
out, nothing "outgroans" their groan for holiness in Heaven.

GROANING CHRISTIANS ARE
GROWING CHRISTIANS

I said at the outset that growing Christians will groan for Heaven
and all it holds. But the reverse is also true—groaning Christians grow.

They set their minds on things above. One of the ways Christians grow is by thinking much about great matters, subjects
that have the power to change their lives. There are no more
powerful or worthy subjects to consider than the Lord Jesus
Christ, Heaven, and the redemption of the body. Growing Christians take seriously, as well as joyously, the command to "seek
those things which are above, where Christ is, sitting at the right
hand of God. Set your mind on things above, not on things on

the earth" (Colossians 3:1-2). Their great Treasure is sitting at the right hand of God. Their greatest hopes and eternal home are among the "things above," so their thoughts are often there also. They'll soon be living there, so they want to visit as often as possible before relocating permanently.

There's no greater example of such heavenly-mindedness than the English Puritan pastor/writer Richard Baxter. He lived during most of the 1600s, though he was in terrible physical condition for nearly all his seventy-six years. He lay sick and lonely in a house far from his home all during the winter of 1646, "sentenced to Death by the Physicians." For his own use he began to write out his meditations about the Heaven he seemed so near to entering. Thus began what may be his most important book, *The Saints' Everlasting Rest.* Believing that his extended thoughts on Heaven were so beneficial, when he recovered he disciplined himself to meditate on Heaven—often while walking—for at least half an hour daily. The final product, published several decades later, was a monumental, still-in-print work that has been one of the most influential Christian books ever written.

The practice of regular "heavenly meditation," as he called it, transformed Baxter and it will transform us. While thirty minutes' meditation on one subject, in addition to the practice of the other spiritual disciplines, may sound unworkable for many in today's culture, we can adopt Baxter's intentionality. Resolving to devote *some* time on a regular basis to reflect upon the coming world and the coming One would encourage, embolden, strengthen, invigorate, illumine, ravish, and de-stress us. And anyone who cannot find time to meditate on Jesus and Heaven is either wasting time or busier than God intends.

The mind never stops. It is like a waterwheel always being turned by the river. Even when we're asleep it is turning, thinking, dreaming. Shouldn't we then put the best thoughts into our minds as much as possible? What better things to think about than Jesus and Heaven?

Groaning Christians purify themselves in anticipation of seeing the Pure One. The apostle John wrote the inspired assurance that when Jesus "is revealed, we shall be like Him, for we shall see Him as He is" (1 John 3:2). Then note what he says about those who groan with this anticipation of seeing the Lord: "And everyone who has this hope in Him purifies himself, just as He is pure" (verse 3). All those ("everyone," not just some) who have this hope, who yearn for the return of Jesus, are affected by it. The second coming of the Lord is not a mere curiosity or just a matter of theological deliberation for them. All those who are sincerely longing to see a *holy* Christ appear are growing more like Christ. How do I know? It's because each one "purifies himself, just as He is pure." In other words, you are in the grip of the groan. Your longings for holiness in Heaven pull you toward holiness now. You can't just wait for holiness; you have to pursue it. As theologian J. I. Packer wrote, "The hope of a holy Heaven, to be enjoyed in the company with our holy Savior, is a potent motive to holiness now."[12]

Do you have "this hope" to "see Him as He is"? How has it affected you? How does it cause you to purify yourself? How are you growing in Christlikeness because of your view of Christ's return?

I am writing these words while on an airplane, just twenty minutes from home after four days and four long flights. The nearer I get to my destination the more I anticipate it. The closer my longing comes to reality the more I think about what and who awaits me. You are nearer the end of your journey than you were when you began this book. Are your thoughts increasingly homeward nowadays? The closer he gets to his heavenly home, the growing Christian will—for the right reasons—think more about what and who awaits him in Heaven. And he will yearn.

NOTES

INTRODUCTION

1. Jonathan Edwards, *The Works of Jonathan Edwards,* vol. 2, Perry Miller, gen. ed., *Religious Affections,* ed. John E. Smith (New Haven, Conn.: Yale University Press, 1959), pp. 346-347. If you find my book helpful and/or would enjoy the challenge of reading a deeper and much more thoughtful one on the same subject, I highly recommend Edwards' *Religious Affections.* It is available in many editions.

CHAPTER 1:
DO YOU THIRST FOR GOD?

1. Jonathan Edwards, *The Works of Jonathan Edwards,* vol. 2, Perry Miller, gen. ed., *Religious Affections,* ed. John E. Smith (New Haven, Conn.: Yale University Press, 1959), p. 104.

2. John Piper, *A Godward Life* (Sisters, Ore.: Multnomah, 1997), pp. 84-85.

3. For further reading on God's desertions, see Joseph Symonds, *The Case and Cure of a Deserted Soul* (1671; reprint ed., Morgan, Penn.: Soli Deo Gloria, 1996).

4. John Blanchard, comp., *Gathered Gold* (Welwyn, England: Evangelical Press, 1984), p. 100.

5. Thomas Shepard, *Parable of the Ten Virgins,* as quoted in Edwards, pp. 376-377.

6. Edwards, p. 379.

7. A. W. Tozer, *The Pursuit of God* (Harrisburg, Penn.: Christian Publications, 1948), p. 8.

8. Tozer, p. 20.

9. For further reading on spiritual mindedness, see Donald S. Whitney, *How Can I Be Sure I'm a Christian?* (Colorado Springs: NavPress, 1994), pp. 67-80.

10. C. H. Spurgeon, "The Panting Heart," *Metropolitan Tabernacle Pulpit*, vol. 14 (1869; reprint, Pasadena, Tex.: Pilgrim Publications, 1982), p. 417.

11. Jonathan Edwards, "Nothing Upon Earth Can Represent the Glories of Heaven," *The Works of Jonathan Edwards*, vol. 14, *Sermons and Discourses, 1723-1729*, ed. Kenneth P. Minkema (New Haven, Conn.: Yale University Press, 1997), p. 143.

12. Edwards, *Sermons and Discourses, 1723-1729*, p. 147.

13. Edwards, *Sermons and Discourses, 1723-1729*, pp. 151-152.

14. Edwards, *Sermons and Discourses, 1723-1729*, pp. 152-153.

15. Edwards, *Religious Affections*, p. 378.

16. Roger Steer, ed., *Spiritual Secrets of George Müller* (Wheaton, Ill.: Harold Shaw, 1985), pp. 62-63.

17. For further reading on scriptural meditation, see Donald S. Whitney, *Spiritual Disciplines for the Christian Life* (Colorado Springs: NavPress, 1991), pp. 43-51, 67-72.

18. Arthur Bennett, ed., *The Valley of Vision* (Edinburgh: The Banner of Truth Trust, 1975).

CHAPTER 2:
ARE YOU GOVERNED INCREASINGLY BY GOD'S WORD?

1. Octavius Winslow, *Personal Declension and Revival of Religion in the Soul* (1841; reprint, Edinburgh: The Banner of Truth Trust, 1993), pp. 17-18.

2. John Piper, *A Godward Life* (Sisters, Ore.: Multnomah, 1997), p. 107.

3. Iain Murray, *Jonathan Edwards: A New Biography* (Edinburgh: The Banner of Truth Trust, 1987), p. 40.

CHAPTER 3:
ARE YOU MORE LOVING?

1. Maurice Roberts, "The Supreme Grace of Christian Love," *The Banner of Truth*, February 1989, p. 3.

2. Jonathan Edwards, *The Works of Jonathan Edwards*, vol. 2, Perry Miller, gen. ed., *Religious Affections*, ed. John E. Smith (New Haven, Conn.: Yale University Press, 1959), p. 146.

3. Edwards, p. 368.

4. Edwards, p. 369.

5. John Piper, *Desiring God* (Portland, Ore.: Multnomah, 1986), p. 96.

6. Jonathan Edwards, *The Works of Jonathan Edwards*, vol. 4, *The Great Awakening*, ed. C. C. Goen (New Haven, Conn.: Yale University Press, 1972), p. 257.

7. Roberts, p. 4.

8. Roberts, p. 4.

9. Wilhelmus à Brakel, *The Christian's Reasonable Service,* vol. 4, trans. Bartel Elshout (Morgan, Penn.: Soli Deo Gloria, 1995), p. 61.

10. Roberts, p. 3.

CHAPTER 4:
ARE YOU MORE SENSITIVE TO GOD'S PRESENCE?

1. George Barna, *Virtual America* (Ventura, Calif.: Regal, 1994), p. 55.

2. Barna, p. 56.

3. Barna, pp. 57-58.

4. Barna, p. 58.

5. I have written more fully on this in "Unity of Doctrine and Devotion," in John H. Armstrong, ed., *The Compromised Church* (Wheaton, Ill.: Crossway, 1998), pp. 241-262.

6. A. W. Tozer, *The Knowledge of the Holy* (New York: Harper & Row, 1961), p. 82.

7. For more on this theme, I recommend a book by a contemporary writer well steeped in the Puritans: Sinclair B. Ferguson, *Deserted by God?* (Grand Rapids, Mich.: Baker, 1993).

8. John Bunyan, *The Pilgrim's Progress* (1678; reprint, Uhrichsville, Oh.: Barbour, 1993), pp. 67-68.

9. John Stevenson, "Prayer: Degrees of Boldness," *The Banner of Truth,* June 1998, p. 21.

10. Martyn Lloyd-Jones, *Enjoying the Presence of God* (Ann Arbor, Mich.: Servant, 1992), p. 133.

11. C. H. Spurgeon, "The Secret of a Happy Life," *Metropolitan Tabernacle Pulpit*, vol. 22 (1876; reprint, Pasadena, Tex.: Pilgrim Publications, 1981), p. 411.

12. Tozer, p. 80.

CHAPTER 5:
DO YOU HAVE A GROWING CONCERN FOR THE
SPIRITUAL AND TEMPORAL NEEDS OF OTHERS?

1. As quoted by W. Stanley Mooneyham in "Orphans," *Baker's Dictionary of Christian Ethics*, ed. Carl F. H. Henry (Grand Rapids, Mich.: Baker, 1973), p. 477.

2. *World* (January 23, 1999), p. 13.

CHAPTER 7;
ARE THE SPIRITUAL DISCIPLINES
INCREASINGLY IMPORTANT TO YOU?

1. For further reading on the personal spiritual disciplines, see Donald S. Whitney, *Spiritual Disciplines for the Christian Life* (Colorado Springs: NavPress, 1991). To learn about the corporate spiritual disciplines, see Donald S. Whitney, *Spiritual Disciplines Within the Church* (Chicago: Moody, 1996).

2. Jonathan Edwards, *The Works of Jonathan Edwards*, vol. 2, Perry Miller, gen. ed., *Religious Affections*, ed. John E. Smith (New Haven, Conn.: Yale University Press, 1959), p. 376.

3. James Gleick, *Faster* (New York: Pantheon, 1999).

4. R. C. Sproul, *The Soul's Quest for God* (Wheaton, Ill.: Tyndale, 1992), p. 7.

CHAPTER 8:
DO YOU STILL GRIEVE OVER SIN?

1. Iain Murray, *Jonathan Edwards: A New Biography* (Edinburgh: The Banner of Truth Trust, 1987), pp. 101-102.

2. Class lecture at Midwestern Baptist Theological Seminary, Kansas City, Missouri, October 22, 1998.

3. John Blanchard, comp., *More Gathered Gold* (Welwyn, England: Evangelical Press, 1986), p. 297.

4. John Blanchard, comp., *Gathered Gold* (Welwyn, England: Evangelical Press, 1984), p. 289.

5. Jonathan Edwards, *The Works of Jonathan Edwards*, vol. 2, Perry Miller, gen. ed., *Religious Affections,* ed. John E. Smith (New Haven, Conn.: Yale University Press, 1959), p. 377.

6. Edwards, p. 366.

7. Jeremiah Burroughs, *The Evil of Evils* (1654; reprint, Ligonier, Penn.: Soli Deo Gloria, 1992), p. 69.

8. Edwards, pp. 316-317.

9. Burroughs, pp. 66-67.

10. John Owen, *The Works of John Owen,* vol. 7, "The Grace and Duty of Being Spiritually Minded" (1850-1853; reprint, Edinburgh: The Banner of Truth Trust, 1965), p. 333.

11. Jerry Bridges, *The Discipline of Grace* (Colorado Springs: NavPress, 1994), pp. 58, 60.

CHAPTER 9:
ARE YOU A QUICKER FORGIVER?

1. John Blanchard, comp., *Sifted Silver* (Durham, England: Evangelical Press, 1995), p. 104.

2. Jay E. Adams, *From Forgiven to Forgiving* (Wheaton, Ill.: Victor, 1989), p. 33.

3. Leon Morris, "Forgiving Others," *Tabletalk*, February 1998, p. 52.

4. John Blanchard, comp., *Gathered Gold* (Welwyn, England: Evangelical Press, 1984), p. 108.

5. John Blanchard, comp., *More Gathered Gold* (Welwyn, England: Evangelical Press, 1986), p. 105.

CHAPTER 10:
DO YOU YEARN FOR HEAVEN AND TO BE WITH JESUS?

1. Jonathan Edwards, ed., *The Life and Diary of David Brainerd*, ed. by Philip E. Howard, Jr. (Chicago: Moody, 1949), p. 87.

2. C. S. Lewis, *Till We Have Faces* (San Diego: Harcourt, Brace & Company, 1984), pp. 74-75.

3. Jonathan Edwards, *The Works of Jonathan Edwards*, vol. 2, Perry Miller, gen. ed., *Religious Affections*, ed. John E. Smith (New Haven, Conn.: Yale University Press, 1959), p. 383.

4. Iain Murray, *Jonathan Edwards: A New Biography* (Edinburgh: The Banner of Truth Trust, 1987), p. 51.

5. John Thornbury, *David Brainerd* (Durham, England: Evangelical Press, 1996), p. 132.

6. Thornbury, p. 132.

7. Joni Eareckson Tada, testimony at the Ligonier Ministries Conference, Orlando, Florida, March 5, 1993.

8. Joni Eareckson Tada, "The Best Part of Heaven," *Moody,* March 1995, p. 32.

9. D. Martyn Lloyd-Jones, *Faith Tried and Triumphant* (Grand Rapids, Mich.: Baker Book House, 1987), p. 199.

10. Murray, p. 143.

11. Edwards, ed., *The Life and Diary of David Brainerd,* p. 88.

12. J. I. Packer, "Why I Like My Pie in the Sky," *Christianity Today,* June 18, 1990, p. 11.

ABOUT THE AUTHOR

DONALD S. WHITNEY is an associate professor of biblical spirituality at the Southern Baptist Theological Seminary in Louisville, Kentucky, and is currently completing a Th.D. at the University of South Africa. He is the author of *Spiritual Disciplines for the Christian Life* and *How Can I Be Sure I'm a Christian?* (all NavPress). Don holds a doctor of ministry degree from Trinity Evangelical Divinity School in Deerfield, Illinois, and was previously a professor of Spiritual Formation at Midwestern Baptist Theological Seminary in Kansas City, Missouri, for ten years. Don's wife, Caffy, ministers from their home as a women's Bible study teacher, an artist, and a freelance illustrator. The Whitneys are parents of a daughter, Laurelen Christiana. You may subscribe to Don's free e-mail newsletter at his website, www.BiblicalSpirituality.org.

THE CHRISTIAN'S JOINT VENTURE WITH GOD.

Trusting God

It's easy to trust God when everything's going your way. But how do you keep faith in God when you have a tragic car accident, lose a job, or discover you have cancer? This book will teach you how to trust God completely, even in the face of adversity. (Jerry Bridges)

The Discipline of Grace

If you've struggled with knowing the difference between your role and God's role in your growth as a Christian, this book on grace is for you Learn to rest in Christ while pursuing a life of holiness. (Jerry Bridges)

The Practice of Godliness

It's easy to get caught up in doing things for God instead of actually being with Him. Learn how to commit yourself to God rather than to activities. (Jerry Bridges)

The Pursuit of Holiness

Holiness should mark the life of every Christian. But holiness is often hard to understand. Learn what holiness is and how to say "no" to the things that hinder it. (Jerry Bridges)